Minimalism

For Families Who Want to Live A More Meaningful Life by Decluttering Their Home
By: Marie Scott

Introduction

True to its name, minimalism is about getting rid of all the unnecessary or unrequired stuff from one's life and making room for all that offers you joy and peace of mind. A minimalistic life involves removing all clutter and consequently leaving you peaceful, free, and light. According to Lao Tzu, one needs to be content with what he or she has. Always be happy with the way things are because when you will realize that you lack nothing, then you will own the whole world.

A minimalist lifestyle is against the idea that more acquisition and consumption is better. It embraces the importance of being content with what we have and what truly makes us happy. Acquiring a lot of things that we really don't need doesn't bring happiness. Trying to have more is quite meaningless.

You need to stop busy all the time to the point that you can't enjoy the pleasures that life offers. A minimalist life values quality as compared to quantity. I practice minimalism, and this is a lifestyle that I really find satisfying. I wake up in a bedroom that has no clutter, have my breakfast, do some reading, and take walks in nature. I also work and spend time with my precious family.

Those are the simple things that offer me happiness. I am not into buying lots of items, traveling a lot, and attending parties. I am also not for spending cash on exorbitant entertainment and watching a lot of TV. The key is to figure out what makes you happy and get rid of the extras so that you can create room for the valuable and important things. Minimalism is not a boring life but rather a rich one in having less.

You don't need to have a minimalist life similar to mine or somebody else. You need to find out what really makes you happy. Always plan your day and get rid of the non-important things while making room for stuff and people you love.

This book will guide you through the path of finding peace and happiness through minimalism. This type of lifestyle is not an end but

Chapter 1: Steps to Minimalism

Even though a majority of people admire the minimalist lifestyle, it is not easy for them to live it. You may want to live this life, but you have no idea what to do or where to start. There are a number of things that you need to think about and do, and that can be quite tedious and overwhelming. Here are a few steps to follow as a beginner:

- *Realize and acknowledge that you have enough.* This is a key point in minimalism because being satisfied with whatever you have is important. Even if you declutter every single day yet you are not content with what you have, you will keep on wanting more.
- *Start decluttering.* You can do this gradually.
- *Simplify your schedule.* Reduce commitments and eliminate things that are not important from your schedule. This will allow you to focus on what's important.
- Edit all that you do.

a route to having more freedom, creating more time, creating room for the important things, worrying less, experiencing more pleasure, being more frugal, and living healthier.

Realize That You Have Enough

This the beginning place, and decluttering is not just enough because you are likely to pile things up again if you continue buying. Therefore, the more you go on acquiring things, the more it means you are not content with how things are at that moment. Buying things you don't need is a clear indication that you lack some kind of satisfaction. You crave for more, and you desire more excitement and ways by which you can spice up your life.

Whatever the reason may be for buying, it is evident that you are not happy with your possessions. This is a problem that can be very addictive; however, don't lose hope. It is recommended that you do the following:

- Make it stick in your mind that you already have whatever you need. The things that you really need are food, clothing, water, shelter, and your loved ones. Everything else is just a bonus. You really don't need to have the latest gadgets, a fancy car, or a big house.
- Kick the habit of buying non-important stuff. Be conscious about it and make a one-month list. Make it a rule that each time you want to buy a non-necessity, you have to jot it down on the list together with the date it was added and that you can't purchase it for at least one month. In case you will need it after one month, then you can still buy it. This technique works because the urge to buy always fizzles out.
- Derive happiness by doing, not owning. Rest assured that you can always be happy by just having the necessities after you realize that owning and having things will never make you happy. On the contrary, doing things can give you happiness. You can talk to a friend, take a walk with a loved one, cook, sing, or do something else that's exciting. Once you realize

that getting involved in activities will make you happy, you will have no desire for excessive stuff.
- Adopt the principle of enough. Have the idea that you don't always need anything extra and that there is a point you always have enough. The problem is that we never know when to stop needing more; it is a vicious cycle. You will be addicted to buying and owning. Learn to have enough and to be happy with what you have. This will take time.

Prioritize Your Necessities

Getting rid of necessities is one of the basics of minimalism. The essence is to create room for what is essential. You don't have to buy new clothes or gadgets if you already have them. You should always learn to be satisfied with the necessary things and carrying out the activities that you enjoy doing. However, it's quite surprising that the things that we most often consider as essentials are never actually necessities.

We group things as essentials since we are used to having them, and it's always difficult to make huge changes. Here are some examples:

- *Cars.* A lot of people view a car as an essential even though mankind survived without them for ages before the twentieth century. Even today, some people still don't use cars, especially if you are in an area or country with some decent and organized public transport system. Moreover, there are carpooling and car-sharing options, which allow you to use a car when you need it without actually owning it. You can rather cycle or walk when you can.
- *Meat.* A majority of us believe that we can't survive without steaks and burgers, including myself before I embraced the minimalist lifestyle. Right now, I am a vegan, and in case you want to join me, start gradually.
- *Clothing.* You don't have to walk naked like the early man or have just one pair of clothing, but buying clothes every other time just to keep up with the trends is not advisable.
- *A huge house.* If you have less, you won't need a big house.

Far from the elimination of physical clutter, minimalism also advocates for the reduction of clutter in one's busy schedule and work life.

This involves doing only what is important so that you can create time for yourself and do what makes you happy.

Cut Down on Commitments

One of the vital things you need to do is to simplify your schedule by listing all your commitments and picking the most essential ones. Commitments refer to all that eats up your time, from work to side jobs. It could even be your leisure activities. Such commitments are quite easy to say yes to, but they occupy a very huge fraction of our lives as they accumulate. This results in us being busy up to the point that we have no time for what is really important to us. If you are keen on practicing minimalism, you need to leave room for what you love the most.

How do you do this? Create a list of every commitment you can think of, and include any activity that you do regularly or one that you have committed to in the short or long term. The next thing is to highlight the five most important commitments. Your top priorities should be the things you love most and are valuable in your life. Everything else should be struck out.

Additionally, you need to make phone calls informing people that you are no longer available for some commitments. This will definitely not be easy because you will have to say no to people and, most of the time, disappoint them. You shouldn't feel guilty for saying no because the lives of other people will go on, as well as their projects. It is never that bad when you disappoint people. This is a slow process of elimination because there are other commitments that you just can't wish away at a glance.

Revise Your Schedule

Reduce the time you spend on meetings, and avoid making appointments that you can ignore. This will leave you with enough time for doing the things that make you happy. You also need to spare some space between things in your schedule as it will help you go through your activities with less stress. If possible, leave some days without scheduled appointments.

Trim your to-do list. Before doing this, be honest with yourself by asking whether you can do all the things in your to-do list today, tomorrow, or even in the coming week. Most of the time, we always believe that we can do more than we actually can. Consequently, we create lengthy to-do lists that we are unable to accomplish within the time we allocate.

Our to-do lists should have fewer tasks that will, in turn, make us not so busy. What this means is that we need to choose the tasks that are most important as well as those that will have the greatest impact on our work and in our lives. Select three task per day, the most important tasks, and make them your tasks of focus before doing any other duties.

Decluttering

Clutter runs parallel to minimalism. If you are serious about minimalism, then you need to remove all the unnecessary items. Decluttering is the core of minimalism. Clutter carries a lot of problems with it such as the following:

- There are items that weigh you down.
- There are things that stress you out.
- It is expensive to buy, store, and maintain items.
- Looking for something in a cluttered space consumes much time.
- It reflects your inner being.

The accumulation of clutter is caused by the desire to acquire instead of being satisfied. Furthermore, cluttering happens due to the fear of not wanting to let things go and the urge to hoard and store things due to the sentimental attachment. When one is too busy, cluttering happens because there is no time for cleaning up and getting rid of the unnecessary stuff. Failure to have a system for dealing with items as well as having no habits of keeping the system also leads to clutter.

You can declutter your house, but if you lack a system and constant habit, you will again start storing things in any place, and once again, there will be clutter. The key is to find a place for everything.

From all that has been said up to this point, it is clear that the barriers to minimalism could be due to unhappiness, stress that leads to wanting more to escape reality, and lack of organization that leads to cluttering. The following chapters will show you how to be organized, avoid stress, and find happiness. Once you unlock the secrets to the three principles, you will be halfway to being a minimalist.

Set Aside a Decluttering Day

Clutter is all the mess around your office, on your desk, in your house, or your closet as a result of you not arranging or putting your stuff in order. Declutter regularly; set aside a day and time every week to clear, arrange, and get your office or house in order. Get rid of items that you do not need, like clothes you are not wearing any longer. Clear your desk of all the papers that are no longer useful.

At all costs, avoid placing things where they do not belong; once a single item is placed in the wrong place, you are set off on a road that is messy. Repeated actions become habits, and habits are really hard to kick. Do not get in the habit of throwing things around and causing a mess. Organized people purge themselves regularly of things that they no longer need to create more room for them and avoid the mess that comes with piling up unnecessary items.

Mind clutter is also an area that you will need to work on; you could easily be suffering from mental chaos! Take time to evaluate your mental state to avoid cluttering your mind. Spend some time to relax and clear your mind of all the unnecessary thoughts and worries that may be clouding your judgment. Do this in conjunction with the other tips cited herein.

Clear every aspect of your life of things that you no longer need; you will lead a much better and organized life devoid of clutter.

Chapter 2: Eliminating Stress as a Minimalist

Lifestyles today are busier and more demanding than ever, and we are inevitably bound to face and deal with the pressures that come with these everyday rigors. Are you feeling more tired lately, or are you struggling to sleep at night when you retire to bed? Do you seem to be more irritable, or are you more anxious? Is it a dreadful affair going to work in the morning?

Rest assured that you are not the only one feeling this way. If you have had such experiences and feelings, then you are most likely manifesting the symptoms of stress. It is also a fact that you cannot lead a minimalist life while under stress. Stress can make you go binge drinking, eating, and even shopping. While under stress, you will tend to do and acquire things that you really don't need just to escape from the realities that stress you. Over time, you will have done and bought a lot of stuff that you really don't need in your life. In fact, most of them are toxic to your health and mind. Stress is a manifestation of our bodies responding to pressures that are exerted on it mentally and physically and is triggered by the body releasing stress chemicals, usually adrenaline, into the bloodstream in the effort to combat pressures that they are faced with.

Stress is unhealthy and should not be allowed to fester and affect our health. It should be confronted as quickly as possible, prevented if possible, and be managed well. Management of stress is relatively easy and can be done quite successfully by making simple adjustments to your lifestyle, picking up and using proven simple techniques to achieve a healthier lifestyle free from stress-cultivating pressures.

So if you find yourself confronted by stress in your daily endeavors, this book will introduce you to simple stress management techniques that have been proven to work in fighting stress. These stress management techniques will help you deal with stress in your daily undertakings at work and at home to aid in calming you down and afford you peace of mind. A stress-free life will leave you happier, more productive, healthy, and with a fresh head to lead a minimalist lifestyle.

I shall delve into and cover a wide range of simple techniques of dealing with life's pressures to reduce mental and physical stress. These techniques are inexpensive, and most can be taken up by anyone of any age without any unwanted side effects.

Apart from the techniques of dealing with stress, we shall get to know the many causes of stress and the signs and symptoms exhibited by those affected by stress. If you are not able to understand and identify that you are ailing from stress, then it would be an exercise in futility to learn the techniques of dealing with it. It is, therefore, a fundamental necessity to understand the condition and be able to easily self-diagnose it.

My hope is to introduce you to these easy techniques of stress management so that you can reap the benefits for a wholesome, healthy, and happy life as a minimalist.

What Is Stress?

Modern lifestyles are demanding and stressful because of the many daily pressures we face. Balancing your personal life and work is not a very easy thing. Between the demands of your job and the needs of your private life, you are bound to face the challenges of stress.

So how exactly would we describe stress?

When our bodies are confronted with a lot of pressure, defensive chemicals or hormones are released into the bloodstream as the body's natural defense. Therefore, stress is the body's response to pressure exerted physically or mentally to it in an attempt to protect itself.

We can classify stress as follows:

1. *Survival stress.* This is experienced when we find ourselves in dangerous situations where one feels at risk of physical harm. This is the type of stress that triggers a fight-or-flight response.
2. *Internal stress.* Internal stress is caused by worries over things that are out of your control. This is self-inflicted stress.
3. *Environmental stress.* This is caused by factors in one's surrounding, like noise.
4. *Tiredness.* Tiredness is caused by fatigue that accumulates over a long period due to things like overworking. Stress is inextricably tied to everyday life, and at one time or another; we are bound to face it. It is not entirely bad as it boosts alertness and concentration; however, it is unhealthy in excess.

Causes, Symptoms, and Effects of Stress

It is important that you know the causes, symptoms, and effects of stress for easy identification and management. When we know what causes stress, we are able to plan and live our lives well away from the stress triggers. Similarly, by being able to tell the respective symptoms, we can recognize the warning signs and act upon them early enough.

Causes of stress:

Stress may be caused by any of the following:

- Major life changes, like divorce, chronic illness, the death of a loved one
- Work burden
- Financial problems
- Trauma
- Constant worry
- Negativity and pessimism
- Fear and anxiety
- Unrealistic expectations

Symptoms of stress:

The following are signs that will let you know that you are suffering from stress:

- Problems remembering things
- Low concentration
- High anxiety
- Constant worry
- Being moody
- Highly irritable and angry
- Loneliness and reclusion
- Sadness

- Low libido
- Aches and pain
- High heart rate
- Dizziness
- Eating disorders—bingeing or self-starving
- Lack of sleep
- Substance abuse
- Nervousness

Stress causes serious social and health problems if not dealt with well.

These are the side effects of stress:

- Mental disorders—depression and anxiety
- Cardiovascular problems—high blood pressure, heart disease, stroke, etc.
- Weight problems—obesity
- Problems with menstrual cycles
- Skin and hair problems—acne, hair loss, etc.
- Sexual dysfunction
- Gastro-intestinal problems—ulcers

Having learned what stress is, as well as its signs and symptoms and the side effects, let us look at the different techniques available for you to deal with this condition.

Meditation for Stress Relief

Meditation is an ancient form of mental and physical transformation of the body through techniques that enhance and develop concentration and positivity. It is a method of deep relaxation that rests the mind and the body. It enables self-regulation of the mind to relax, attain clarity, and build positive internal energy. There are many types and techniques of meditation. The most common are the following:

- Yoga
- Tai chi
- Zen meditation (Zazen)

Meditation is a proven stress reliever and is being prescribed and taken up by many to calm down. Stress relief requires mental and physical relaxation, and meditation provides that. So how will meditation help you deal with stress?

- *Deep breathing.* This is a simple and quick relaxer. More oxygen is absorbed in the body, thus better functionality.
- *Mental balance.* For optimal functioning of the body, the nervous system must be at equilibrium. Remember that stress destabilizes this balance.

Meditation leads to positive change in the body; cells are injected with more energy, which boosts overall functioning leading to inner peace, happiness, and motivation. These are the benefits of meditation:

- Meditation reverses or reduces the production of stress hormones, making you calm to prevent chronic stress. When stress hormones are subdued or controlled, the body will be more relaxed.

- It aids in the management of blood pressure and other cardiovascular conditions by slowing down breathing and heart rate.
- The immune system is boosted through the suppression of destructive stress chemicals.
- Meditation enhances mental clarity and creativity.
- Meditation promotes a pure life; in fact, it aims for the attainment of purity akin to the higher being. It will encourage you to quit poisonous habits, like smoking, drug abuse, and excessive alcohol consumption.
- It improves brain functioning by boosting psychological creativity, which results to having a better memory and a relaxed mind.
- It makes you happier. A relaxed person worries less.
- You sleep better, enabling you to rest more and face the day and tasks.
- Reduces the aging process through mental and physical exercise and suppression of stress hormones. Stress hormones hasten the aging process.
- Meditation will improve your metabolism and help regulate body weight.
- Meditation leads to emotional balance and harmony.

Meditating very early in the morning is considered more beneficial; you are well rested and your surrounding is serene and ideal for meditation. We shall discuss meditation in depth in the next chapter.

Run the Stress Off

Running is a great way of combating stress. It is one of the easiest and beneficial physical exercises anyone can engage in. If you are feeling beat down by the rigors of life, take a run down your street or get to the nearest field and run a few laps. There are several benefits that you will experience if you run regularly:

- Running, which is an aerobic exercise, increases the heart rate and makes you sweat. It stimulates the release of endorphins, which are the body's natural feel-good chemicals, leaving your brain elated and making you happy.
- You will shed calories, which will help with lowering your blood pressure and keeping your arteries in good shape.
- Running slows the aging process and reduces bone and muscles loss by building strength and flexibility. It keeps you active and improves your overall health.
- When running, you have all the time to yourself, which allows you to process your thoughts. You may use the time to aid you with sorting out some issues that you may be facing or to think through a problem.
- Researchers have found out that people who are regular runners lead a happier, more stress-free life and are generally fitter than those who do not. Your concentration and alertness are also enhanced.

Now, put on those running shoes and hit the road for a healthier, happier, and stress-free life. Running can be done almost anywhere you go. You do not have to worry about where to perform this exercise. It is recommended that you drink a lot of water if you are a runner. Drink at least a liter of water an hour to two hours before your run. This helps hydrate the body, and you are unlikely to suffer dehydration. You will not regret your decision as the benefits that will accrue to you are many.

Take a Hike

Hiking is a relaxing walk through a natural environment, usually at a nature trail, a park, or a forest. Much like running, hiking is a great exercise for stress relief, though less vigorous. Hiking combines the benefits of an effective aerobic exercise, natural serene surrounding, and the chance and time to relax and think freely. The following are ways hiking helps the body to deal with stress:

- *Mental relaxation.* Hiking provides the time and opportunity for mind relaxation by getting you up close to nature. Nature has been proven as a catalyst to mental relaxation by giving you the experience and wonders of natural surroundings.
- *Energizing the body.* Hiking, being an aerobic exercise, invigorates the body and helps with the regulation of stress chemicals. People who hike regularly have higher levels of feel-good hormones, like endorphins, which reduce stress considerably.
- *Emotional well-being.* When you are stressed, you are a prisoner of negative emotions, like sadness, anxiety, nervousness, etc. Hiking will activate positive energy in your body, which will, in turn, boost your emotions to make you feel better and happier.
- *Brain exercising.* A hike will afford you the silence and time to think profoundly about things that are important to you. Aerobic exercise, coupled with deep thinking, will effectively enhance the body's stress management capabilities.
- *Spiritual nourishment.* Being in a natural environment with the wonderful serenity offers the body a chance to get spiritually fulfilled. Your nerves will be calmed, and you will get the opportunity for mental clarity and relaxation that you would normally not have every day.

Hiking is a great exercise for stress relief, and you ought to prepare in advance before you go on a hike. Pack a first-aid kit, drinking water, and a phone in case you may be confronted with an accident. Come on, why don't you start hiking for a change? It may just be the answer to dealing with the stress you have been under lately. So book an appointment with nature for exercise—it is the key to mental and spiritual fulfillment—and say goodbye to stress.

Pedal the Stress Away

Do you remember how happy you were riding your bicycle when you were young? I remember my experience, and I could give anything to feel the same way again—exciting, happy, and a sense of unbridled freedom. It was just a great time without a care in the world.

Well, you do not have to look back to your childhood with such nostalgia because you can readily bring back those feel-good moments you had on your bicycle then to the present to replace all the anxiety and worries you are facing now! Don't you want to?

Cycling is another form of aerobic exercise that is great for stress relief, fitness, and general well-being. When you are overwhelmed by life's pressures, simply hop on a bike and start pedaling for stress relief. Being on the bike will take your mind off the problems that are bothering you. It will pump some feel-good chemicals into your bloodstream and leave your heart feeling refreshed and emotionally elated.

You can cycle after work or on weekends or during your day off. You can even cycle to work. And while doing this, employ the meditative technique of mantra by chanting a positive phrase or word to the rhythm of your pedaling. I assure you that you will be surprised at how fast your mind will be cleared of the negativity and stress that you are facing.

Cycling is not an expensive endeavor. Just buy a bicycle, and you may start. It is not vigorous if done for leisure or exercise, and it can be taken up by people of all ages. Cycling will keep you fit. Work out your heart for better health and emotional balance. It helps with the management of chronic conditions, like diabetes, cardiovascular problems, and high blood pressure.

The healthier and better you feel, the less likely you are to be stressed. Get on your bike and enjoy the stress-relieving benefits you have been missing.

Reading for Stress Relief

Reading is cathartic and is a great reliever of stress for people who are facing everyday pressures and adversity. It relaxes the brain and manages the thought process. When you read, your mind travels away from the pressures you are facing. You sink into the story where you will find yourself in faraway worlds. In the duration of your reading, you shall be transported away from your troubles, and this helps to balance your emotional well-being.

Reading is a great mental exercise that stimulates brain activity, thereby improving mental concentration and alertness. Stress-fighting chemicals that give you a happy feeling are released into the brain. An active mind is strong and more likely to cope with daily pressures. You will also fight stress from the motivation and hope you derive from reading biographies and motivational books. Books and other literature are sources of information that enables you to learn more and aid in problem-solving.

A book will divert your thoughts from the lingering problems or worries that are stressing you out. Set aside a few hours in your day to read, and you will experience how fulfilling it can be in your efforts at dealing with stress.

When you clear your mind of negativity even for a few hours, you will make huge strides in mental relaxation. With a relaxed mind, you should be able to be more creative and relaxed, enabling you to cope with stress. An active mind also slows down the aging process, leaving you feeling younger physically and mentally. A strong healthy body is less prone to stress.

If the last time you read was for an exam or for a school assignment, make a hot cup of tea, make yourself comfortable on your favorite seat, and immerse yourself into a book. The benefits for your life and health are great; you need to try it. Get literature that appeals to you. Whether it is a book, magazine, or newspaper, make it a habit to read regularly for a less-stressful life every day.

Be a Positive Thinker

Have you heard of positive thinking? Well, the world works in a very simple way in that whatever you think is what will be manifested in your life. You attract what you think!

It may seem simplistic or difficult to accept, but take the time to mull it over, and you will realize that it is true. If you want to get that new job you applied to or if you want to get promoted, it begins by your wanting it, then believing that you can get it without having a shred of doubt. Self-belief is a powerful stress reliever. Be positive and to be ever optimistic.

The power of positive thinking is incredible; if you look forward to good things, you will have a happier, less-stressful life. Positive thinking is a state where you look forward to favorable outcomes in whatever you do. Positive thinking, therefore, involves actively training your mind to have creative thoughts that transform energy into reality. Avoid dwelling on your failures, and concentrate on the successes. Use the disappointments as lessons for the future.

Studies show that positive thinking leads to a longer and healthier life since you are less prone to stress. You become a positive thinker by identifying the negative aspects of your thinking, and avoid them while constantly evaluation your thoughts to make sure you stay on the positive. Do not be too hard on yourself. Allow yourself joyous moments, and take time to have fun. Surround yourself with like-minded people who will help you build the habit of positive thinking.

When you are optimistic, you become less critical and are instead more creative and hopeful. An optimistic mindset is able to deal with stress at work more easily and constructively. Positive thinking is a powerful tool in fighting stress. Try it, and you are sure of great benefits of living a happy, relaxed life.

Time Management

If you are always late and short of time, then you are most likely leading a stressed life. There is nothing as stressful as the struggle to always meet a deadline or catch up with something you forgot about. Properly using the little time we have will help you cope with stress.

Time management involves methods aimed at using time efficiently to perform all the tasks we have within a given time. It involves prioritizing, scheduling, and organizing. You must assess the tasks on your plate and put them in order of importance and urgency to avoid confusion, conflicts, and unnecessary time pressures.

Plan things in advance to avoid last-minute scrambling in an effort to get something that skipped your mind done. Good time management makes you a more productive person. You will do more within a short time, thus gaining more control of your life. Create a schedule and stick to it. You will have enough free time to engage in fun things that you have been missing. You will have time to go to the movies, play a game, or do any other fun activity that serves to boost health and well-being.

Good time management means that you have enough time for work, family, and friends. These moments with loved ones are most fulfilling and stress-relieving.

It does not take much to be a good time manager; all you need is start and commit to it. Well-managed time leads to a more comfortable and happy life. Here are the benefits of time management for a less-stressful life:

- Doing more with less time.
- Getting more free time that allows time to relax.
- Stress is reduced since you do not worry about pending deadlines.
- Higher productivity—you are fresh mentally and physically

and highly motivated.

Time management is good because you will be happier, more successful, more productive, live a fuller and stress-free life. Why don't you start managing your time better and enjoy the benefits?

Get Enough Sleep

Are you sleeping enough? Lack of adequate sleep is a big contributor to incidences of stress. Getting sufficient sleep is essential in your effort to deal with stress; during sleep the body gets a chance to rest, to heal, and to be rejuvenated. When you do not get enough sleep, you are left susceptible to stress and other health problems because you are emotionally imbalanced.

Therefore, it is imperative to have a sleeping schedule and follow it so that you condition your body into a routine for sufficient rest. In fact, sleep deficiency is a great source of stress since you are tired, irritable, and have weakened creativity. Between work and your personal affairs, you probably end up not getting enough sleep.

It is recommended that you sleep for six hours for optimal rest. However, many of us do not meet this target as studies show that most of us sleep for as little as two hours and a maximum of four hours in a twenty-four-hour cycle! We do not get sufficient sleep because of our poor bedtime habits that end up interfering with our sleep. To sleep better and longer, try the following:

- Set a sleeping schedule; you will sleep better if your bedtime is predictable. Your body will adapt and you will rest more.
- Do not indulge in a heavy meal for supper; have a light meal at least two hours before you retire to bed.
- Physical exercise is a great sleep inducer; work out three to four hours before you sleep.
- Do not take caffeinated drinks close to your bedtime; your last caffeine drink should be averagely six hours or more before you lie down.
- Keep away from alcohol four to six hours before your bedtime; it will disrupt your sleep.

Sleep well for emotional balance; you will wake up refresh, well rested, and energized. When your body has this balance, it can easily manage or ward off stress.

Listening to Soothing Music

Music is very relaxing and has the ability to change moods positively by acting on our minds to avert stress. It acts quickly, is available, and will relieve you of stress. The calming effect of music has a distinctive relationship with our emotions. Music is an effective way to cope with stress. Slow classical music is extremely peaceful and has a positive effect on our bodies and minds. This kind of music has its advantages; it slows the heart and pulse rates, reduces the production of stress hormones, and lowers the blood pressure.

Music engrosses our thoughts to distract us from whatever worries that may be lingering in our minds. Most times when you are stressed, your mind tends to wander off, causing you to think of the things that cause you more anxiety. However, music acts as a cushion and helps your mind to relax and better concentrate.

For years, music has been proven to treat ailments and restore coherence and balance between your body and mind. Furthermore, research has it that music is therapeutic in the following ways:

- Some music compositions can help disabled people by boosting harmonization and communication and improve their life.
- The use of headphones when listening to music can lessen anxiety and stress, especially when one is about to go for surgery and after the surgery.
- During extreme pain or post-surgery, music has been known to ease and numb the pain.
- Music is also known to alleviate depression and enhance self-esteem in older people.
- Soothing music has been proven to improve mood and reduce burnout.
- Music is therapeutic, especially for cancer patients. It

improves the quality of life and reduces emotional trauma.

Music is food for the soul; the next time you are facing adversity or are feeling down from mental fatigue or some other worries, turn on your favorite music. Enjoy the relaxing and positive vibes that will be provided by the music.

Share Your Problems; Talk to Someone

A problem shared is a problem solved or half solved. Sharing our problems is therapeutic and a quick fix to stress. Putting a lid on your suffering and keeping it to yourself is an emotional burden and is very unhealthy. Many of us are fiercely independent and would want to solve our problems on our own. However, there is a point where you are better off talking to someone about what you are going through.

Pent-up emotions and suffering will turn you into a very stressed and imbalanced person. Reach out to someone you trust—a friend or relative—for a listening ear and realize the great positive impact it will have on you. Talking to someone has the following benefits:

- Sharing your problems will help you get rid of bad emotions, like worries, anxiety, etc. You will feel better after since you will have let go of the emotional burden.
- Your pain is reduced since you will have someone sharing your problem and empathizing with you.
- Solutions to your problems are easier to come by as you will be readily advised by the listener.
- By sharing, you lead a healthier life since you negate the effects of emotional distress caused by pent-up emotional turmoil.
- You will simply feel better and happier at having talked about whatever is bothering you.

By sharing, we get the load off our chests, leaving us emotionally boosted, relaxed, and stronger. It also prevents the situation from deteriorating to a deeper problem, like depression or emotional breakdown. With a relaxed, more-stable mental state, you have the clarity and strength to handle your problem and will easily embark on problem-solving for a stress-free life.

From now on, if you find yourself in a tight place emotionally and are feeling stressed, seek someone you can share your problem with, and enjoy the quick stress relief that comes with it.

You Should Laugh More

The benefits of laughter in coping with stress and for a healthier life are numerous. It is proven that humor is a powerful tool for stress relief. Try to laugh and be cheerful despite the tough times. Laughter has a way of rubbing off on others. So if you are happy, those around you will follow, and you will be surrounded by happiness. A happy life is a stress-free life. Laughter enhances oxygen intake and stimulates the functioning of body organs, like the heart, brain, and lungs. Your heart rate is also improved for better blood flow and cardiovascular well-being.

By laughing your way through life, you benefit from muscles relaxation and tension relief. Your immunity will be enhanced through the release of stress-fighting chemicals in the body. All the pain you are suffering emotionally and even physically is reduced by laughter, which triggers the production of the body's natural pain-killing hormones. A happy person is a magnet attracting people for improved social life and emotional state.

So when you are downcast, just smile through it, and you will feel better. In any case, the difficulties will soon pass, and with a positive and happy approach, you will survive it. Laughter subdues toxic stress-attracting thoughts, helps you forget your worries, and enables you to concentrate and work on the tasks at hand. Be happy and grateful for the good things you have been blessed with; think about them when you are stressed. Laugh and smile as you recollect, and be assured of a stress-free life.

A good sense of humor is not a panacea, but it sure improves your outlook in life, your health, and your social standing. A good laugh will do you a lot of good. Smile and laugh more. Laughter is indeed the best medicine.

Eat Healthy Foods

Food is the fuel and the source of nourishment for the body. It is an integral part of our general well-being and good health. It is important that we eat the right foods and eat well for us to stay healthy. A healthy body is able to fend off the side effects of stress with ease.

Food and stress are uniquely interwoven; when faced with adversity, some people have a sudden craving for food while others will lose their appetite. It is, therefore, necessary that we know the right foods to eat, especially when we are under some sort of stress. When we encounter stress, we crave comfort foods, such as fats and sugars. These foods are not healthy. It will cause harm to us and will cause us more stress. To stay healthy and manage stress, we have to avoid the following:

- Consuming a lot of fast foods. They are unhealthy and more expensive than cooking for yourself in the long run.
- Skipping meals. It is a catalyst for stress. If you miss meals, you are likely to be fatigued and less nourished, thus susceptible to stress.
- Having too much caffeinated drinks. This interferes with your sleep and denies you adequate rest.
- Eating the wrong food types. Eat a balanced diet and resist the temptation of eating too much of foods rich in fats and sugars. These foods only led to weight gain and cardiovascular problems.

A poor diet will leave you with problems of hormonal imbalance and weight problems (either you're losing or gaining too much). You will develop a weak immune system and are likely to be susceptible to illnesses. Unhealthy eating will also lead to an imbalance of the blood sugar, which may lead to diabetes.

Stress makes your body burn nutrients. You consume much faster than normal; that is why you should be on a healthy diet. It is wise that you replenish these nutrients to help cope with stress.

Work-Life Balance

All work with no play makes Jack a dull boy! This old saying is very true; you need to have some time away from your job to have fun and engage in things that excite you and pump your blood.

Most adults who are stressed can trace the source to their workplace because we spend a lot of time on the job. It is, therefore, important to balance the time we spend working and time for ourselves for a healthier lifestyle. Work-life balance is about dividing your time effectively and adequately between work and your private life. If you let work consume most of your time and neglect or shortchange your personal needs, you will end up stressed. When your personal life is in order, you are less likely to be stressed since you will worry less. Your mind will not be stretched from being divided between what you need to do at work and the personal matters awaiting your attention.

Spend time with family and friends; it is relaxing and healthy for you. When was the last time you went cycling or shopping with your children? These mundane activities are the foundation to a well-balanced healthy life devoid of stress. If your private life brings you happiness, you will be able to face pressures that come your way.

After spending time with your loved ones, you need to set aside personal time for things that are self-gratifying. Go for a massage or run a few laps at the neighborhood field. Volunteer your services for a worthy cause. Such acts are great for boosting your emotional well-being. If you embrace a healthy work-life balance, you will reap the many benefits. Personal nourishment and care is important for overall health. Balance your private and professional life for a stress-free healthy life where you are happier and revitalized.

Write; Pick Up Your Pen and Paper

Another technique of dealing with stress is writing; it is especially encouraged when one is so stressed or depressed. Putting down your experience, feelings, and thoughts in a journal is very therapeutic for recovery and for defeating stress.

Writing works by clarifying your mind and thoughts, and it is a form of therapy in the sense that it compels you to recall events and thoughts of the day on paper to give you a better avenue to analyze and understand what happened. It is also meditative because it slows down your heart as you focus on your writing, streaming out your thoughts to paper.

Writing sharpens and stimulates brain functioning and activity to improve your mental acuity and concentration, as well as improving your vocabulary. You are, therefore, better equipped to handle stressful situations. When you write regularly, the stress triggers in your head are disrupted, allowing you to better relax and sleep better. You get up well rested and energized. Writing also fights anger by removing the thoughts from your mind to the writing pad, essentially offering you a platform to vent it out.

When you write down your worries and problems, it is easier to solve them; writing allows you to identify what the problem is. Think it through over time, and most likely, come up with a great unrushed solution to avert the stress that you may have. Having a to-do list or schedule helps you focus and get organized. You are able to plan in advance to avoid last-minute rush or procrastination, which will only serve to make your life stressful.

Writing will boost your immune system; by slowing your breathing, you are able to breathe in more oxygen to better nourish the brain and blood, leading to faster healing and an enhanced ability to fight pathogens. Better breathing also strengthens the lungs, which has a positive effect in fighting respiratory conditions like asthma.

To reap the benefits of writing for better health and stress relief, it does not matter what you write. The main thing is to be able to jot down your thoughts and review them. You do not have to be a John Grisham! Write down what is on your mind because the healing power lies in you, letting out the negative thoughts that are weighing on your mind.

Chapter 3: Minimalism Meditation

Several religions advocate for meditation. An example is Buddhism and the way their monks practice a minimalist lifestyle. Monks only utilize needs and necessities, not wants. They live their lives at a minimum and meditation is one of the tools that aid in their reflection, contentment and simplicity in life. The word meditation originates from the Latin word meditation, and it means to think, ponder, or contemplate.

Meditation is a way of transforming the mind and body through techniques that enhance and develop concentration and positivity. It is a method of deep relaxation that rests the mind and, in turn, the body. Simply put, meditation is peace of mind!

The aim of meditation is to achieve self-regulation of the mind by using the various meditation techniques for relaxation, mental clarity, and building positive internal energy. It is this end that helps manage health problems, like anxiety, depression, and high blood pressure. The body is nourished and healed through rest. Deep rest and relaxation achieved through meditation is, therefore, great for rejuvenating the body to leave you well and mentally serene.

Research has shown that the degree of rest achieved when one is meditating is greater than that harnessed from sleep. The findings are incredible; twenty minutes of deep meditation has been equated to seven hours of sleep! The desired goal of mental clarity, positivity, and peace is reached through regular practice of meditative techniques. For maximum harvest of the benefits, be committed to this art; in the course of time, your body will get into a rhythm and in tune for inner peace.

Brief History

Meditation has a long and rich history; this mental- and physical-wellness art is dated as far back as some of the old civilizations and religions. Meditation is closely interlinked to religion in many places where it is traditionally practiced, and it may have its roots in religion.

Meditation techniques were employed for the attainment of a higher purpose in the pursuit of divine perfection—to bring one closer to the creator. Research has it that the earliest evidence of meditation is in Hindu scriptural texts. It is from these beginnings that other forms of meditation developed in Asia and the Orient. In the sixth and fifth century, meditation has been adopted in China by Taoists and Hindus, Jains, and Buddhists in India.

In Islam, Sufism, and Dhikr practice meditation through word repetitions, chants, movements, and controlled breathing.

In the West, Christian meditation picked up around the sixth century during Bible readings among Benedictine monks. Modern forms of meditation that most of us practice today appeared in India in the 1950s as secular forms of meditation techniques that are more geared toward reduction of stress, self-improvement, and relaxation. The modern forms of meditation do not focus on spirituality.

In fact, meditation was used by these religions as techniques for bringing practitioners closer to God, for the closer one was to God, the more peaceful they were and the more clarity of mind they attained. With the brief history and knowledge of meditation, let us look at the different types and techniques of meditation practiced around the world in the next.

Types or Techniques of Meditation

Several types and techniques of meditation are in use, therefore, it is not possible to include every detail within this chapter. Meditative techniques are in the hundreds but are all linked by the common thread of aiming at achieving inner peace for the practitioner.

First and foremost, all meditative practices engage in mind-control techniques as a way to achieve relaxation and peace. Secondly, there are postures and body movements that are found in all forms of meditation. These two traits are evident in all meditative practices pointing to a common goal for all of them. Meditation helps relieve our bodies and minds of the toxic effects of stress. It relaxes us and brings the peace of mind that we all yearn for.

Prior to selecting your preferred meditation style or technique, it is imperative that you carry out a comprehensive research and demystify everything about them. Interrogate yourself. Find out and decide what your meditative goals are or would be to help you pick up the right technique for you. In some cases, you will need to get a teacher or join a meditation school for the right advice, coaching, and mentorship in taking up meditation.

There are types of meditative practices that cannot be performed by beginners, people with certain conditions or illnesses, or older people for example. Seeking the right information will guide you to the right technique.

It will also serve you well if you select a meditation style or technique that is in sync with your lifestyle. Meditation requires consistency, regularity, discipline, and high commitment for one to realize the desired fruits. With the many types of meditation in existence, we can generally categorize meditation as follows:

- *Concentrative meditation.* In concentrative meditation, the mind is directed to a particular object, chant/mantra, sound

or sensation. The practitioner will focus their mind and energy on a focal point of their choosing that best works for them in an effort to clear and calm their minds and bodies. In case you are a starter, this is the best meditation technique that suits you.
- *Mindfulness meditation.* This type of meditation does not rely on focusing the mind on an object but relies on feelings, sensations, emotions, and thought patterns to achieve a meditative state. This is a more advanced type of meditation that is not for everyone, especially beginners.
- *Effortless transcending.* This meditation technique is also known as "effortless" because it does not involve any mental effort or concentration. Some people also refer to this meditation technique as "pure being" or "transcendental". This is because it centers on being empty, introverting, and keeping calm. The goal is to eliminate all thoughts and allow a person to identify his or her real importance and true nature. With consistent practice, the mind becomes an open space that allows for relaxation. It has been compared to massaging the brain. The supernatural procedure will aid you in keeping your mind quiet. Consequently, you will be conscious of an extensive condition of alertness. People who exercise this kind of meditation technique may go through a state of feeling empty or non-existence. Additionally, this state brings a good feeling.

What follows are meditation techniques.

Buddhist Meditation

- *Zen meditation (Zazen).* Zazen is a Japanese term meaning "seated Zen" or "seated meditation," referring to the form of Zen meditation practiced while sitting. Zazen originates from Chinese Zen Buddhism. It is done while seated on the floor, usually on a mat, with crossed legs. This was traditionally done in the lotus or half-lotus position. For the mind, Zazen employs two techniques:

1. Focus on breathing. The practitioner will pay attention to inhalation and exhalation while silently counting down with every breath and back.
2. Shikantanza: Here there is no specific object of meditation. One remains in the moment being aware of what goes through their mind and what passes around.

- *Vipassana meditation.* Vipassana means clear seeing or insight and is a Buddhist type of meditation. It is ideal for mental discovery and awareness. It starts with mindfulness of breath to stabilize and focus the mind—focused-mind meditation. Then it moves to develop clarity and awareness of bodily sensations and mental phenomena. Sit on the floor, legs crossed with a straight back.
- *Mindfulness meditation.* Mindfulness meditation combines practices from various Buddhist meditation practices. It is widely employed in hospitals and other health benefits as a form of treatment. Here, the practitioner will focus on the moment while not losing awareness of the thoughts and emotions experienced.
- *Religious/spiritual meditation.* These are meditative practices that are practiced among the different religions; remember

that spirituality is one avenue for achieving peace of mind and relaxation. Here meditation and prayer are combined to achieve spiritual development by reflection of God's word. Meditation is a communion with the self with the aim of spiritual development or divinity. Meditation in religion is practiced for peace of mind by steadying and focusing it to give the practitioner the ability for divine insight.

A practitioner of Christian meditation said that God is sought through the study of scripture, but through meditation, he is found. There are forms of meditative practices in almost all religions that prove the close link between spirituality and meditation. Sufism meditative practices are some of the most elaborate of religious meditation. Practitioners get into a rhythm of chanting and movement that eventually transports participants into a spiritual realm. In Christianity, there are examples with the Catholics and Orthodox sects that have mantras or repetitive prayers.

Metta Meditation

This meditation style is also known as loving-kindness meditation, and it traces its origin in Tibet. This meditative form enhances empathy and compassion to make one more loving to self and others. The practitioner will sit and close their eyes, then generate feelings of kindness and compassion in their mind toward themselves then progress to others.

Just like the name suggests, this type of meditation aims at creating harmony with one's surrounding. Treat all things with kindness, and the rewards are happiness and compassion for you. You emit happiness, and the world bounces it back to you.

Hindu Meditations

Vedic and Yogic forms of meditation are Hindu forms and are classified as follows:

- *Mantra meditation.* Mantra involves the repetition of a word or phrase to focus one's mind.
- *Transcendental meditation.* Transcendental techniques aim at opening the mind
- *Yoga meditation.* Yoga means "union," and it exists in different forms. Yoga combines mind relaxing and focusing practices with stretching movements and postures. Of all the meditative practices, yoga is the most popular of the secular forms of meditation and has the most following for nonreligious or spiritual meditation. You will find that most people who meditate are practicing one form of yoga or another. How then do we use these techniques for self-improvement and relaxation? Let us first know the benefits of meditation.

Benefits of Meditation

There are several benefits apart from the ones we have discussed in the preceding chapters; it is no wonder then that meditation is being promoted as an alternative to clinical treatment for cure and management of several health conditions and for general well-being. Meditation leads the body to undergo a change. Cells in the body are injected with more energy, resulting in peace, happiness, and motivation as the energy levels in the body are boosted. Here are the benefits of meditative practices:

1. Meditation reverses or reduces the production of stress hormones (adrenaline) by creating calmness and eradicating anxiety to prevent chronic stress. With controlled or regulated stress hormones, the body is more relaxed.
2. It is good for managing blood pressure and other heart diseases or conditions since the heart rate and breathing is slowed down. When we are not stressed, worried, or anxious, the heart rate is slow. As a result, one's blood pressure also reduces. Meditation can help greatly with conditions like high blood pressure since it works to create calmness and relaxation.
3. Boosts the immune system and slows aging as a result of less production of adrenaline by the body. The immune system is boosted since one ends up being healthier as a result of the suppression of destructive stress chemicals.
4. Meditation brings clarity of the mind, and creativity is enhanced. With a relaxed mind, one is sure to be more creative and productive.
5. Meditative techniques advocate for a pure life, and in fact, the aim of meditation is to attain purity akin to the higher being, so practitioners find themselves quitting poisonous

habits, like smoking, drug abuse, and alcohol consumption.
6. Brain functioning is greatly improved through the boosting of psychological creativity, a better memory, and a settled relaxed mind.
7. Meditation makes you happier since your mind and body feel better. A relaxed person has no worries and will be a happier person.
8. You will sleep better since you are relaxed, enabling you to have better rest to face the day and your tasks.
9. Meditation reduces how fast we age through mental and physical exercise. People who meditate have a slower aging process. Stress hormones hasten aging while meditation is known to halt or significantly reduce their production.
10. Meditation reduces or eliminates stress. A meditation practitioner is a calm and happy individual who is essentially immune to the effects of stress.
11. A relaxed and happier person has the benefit of a better-functioning body; immunity is boosted and diseases are kept at bay.
12. When one embraces meditation with all its tenets and understands it, they hold life to a greater value since they learn the true meaning and purpose of living.
13. Meditative exercises improve metabolism and help regulate weight by fighting obesity.
14. Meditation helps you feel more connected and in tune with yourself.
15. Meditation brings emotional balance and harmony.
16. Personal transformation is inevitable with meditation. The end result is you transforming into a new being.

It is recommended that you meditate at least once a day for optimal results. Dawn meditation is highly recommended usually between 3:00

a.m. and 6:00 a.m. Meditation at dawn is regarded as more helpful because it makes you more alert and well relaxed after a night's sleep. The environment is also quiet and ideal for meditation.

Using Meditation to achieve Relaxation

Relaxation is a state of mental and physical calmness and serenity where one is free from tension and anxiety. Meditation practices reduce muscle tension, lower blood pressure, calm the mind, and eliminate stress in general.

A response christened "relaxation response" is elicited when one is relaxed. It contradicts the stress response that one undergoes when one is under coercion. Meditation is one sure way of generating the relaxation response. Regular meditation will generate relaxation response, giving you more control of your body for a stress-free life. The following are the most-used relaxation techniques:

- *Progressive muscle relaxation.* This method is used for the purposes of relaxing deep muscle tension. Tension in the muscles increases anxiety, and this technique will reduce muscle tension and lower the heart rate and blood pressure. It can be practiced while lying on your back or seated. You tense each muscle group for a few seconds and then relax. This is repeated until the whole body relaxes.
- *Deep breathing.* Deep breathing emphasizes breathing control and focusing on your breathing to achieve a relaxed state. Take deep breaths from the stomach, breathing in enough air into your lungs. Having deep breaths means more oxygen into your system. More oxygen means less tension and anxiety. Deep breathing is a simple but powerful relaxation technique that is easily learned by all and can be done almost anywhere. It offers a quick fix for managing stress levels. Remember that deep breathing is the basis of other relaxation techniques and can be applied together with other relaxation tools, like aromatherapy and music. You can use the following routine for your deep breathing meditative technique:

1. Have a seat with your back straightened. With one hand on your chest with the other placed on your tummy. Your hands are the ones to lead you through the process of breathing.
2. Breathe in using your nose; the hand resting on your belly will be shoved upwards while the one on your thorax will experience very little motion.
3. Breathe outwards using the mouth, and expel as much air as possible. Tighten your belly muscles while you are at it. The hand placed on your stomach will move inward as you breathe out while the other hand will hardly move.
4. Continue breathing in using your nose and exhaling through your mouth. Breathe in sufficient air so that your lower tummy rises and drops.
5. Count down slowly as you breathe out.
6. If breathing from your abdomen is a problem while you are seated, lie on a flat surface—the floor is ideal.
7. Let a light and visible object rest on your belly. It should act as a guide when you breathe. The object should move up as you breathe in air and lower as you exhale.

- *Tense/relax method.* This technique is similar to progressive relaxation where you tense and relax muscles for relaxation.
- *Autogenic method.* The autogenic method is also about muscle control to make one calmer and relaxed.
- *Guided imagery or envision technique.* This can be used in conjunction with progressive relaxation or by itself. After you have relaxed your muscles, you can get into the visualization method and use mental imagery to relax your mind. Visualization method is a variation on traditional forms of meditation techniques. It requires the use of all senses—sight, taste, touch, hearing, and smell. Visualization method entails the creation of an image in your mind, leaving you feeling at

peace and free to release all tension and anxiety.
- *Self-hypnosis.* This refers to a kind of a piloted meditation that is about hearing to a recording so as to achieve an extended relaxed condition. As soon as you reach a condition of extended relaxation, you will be more open to suggestion, giving the hypnotherapist the chance to focus on a specific facet of thought for its improvement.
- *Standard meditation.* There are many types of standard guided meditations, many having different aims and purposes. Guided meditations are not the same, so you ought to know which one you are using and for what purpose is it.
- *Body scan.* This is a piloted meditation technique in which a recording offers instructions to a person to anchor on a certain body part and pin point any tension. Scanning of the body involves increased perception of any stress or pain in selected body parts. You can scan your body while sitting or lying down in a comfortable situation. Scanning of the full body takes a long time (up to one hour), even though shorter varieties still have a stronger impact.
- *Brainwave meditation.* This type of meditation targets brain waves for stress relief and relaxation. Brain-wave meditations start out with a guiding voice, which is usually just relaxing music and sounds. The aim is to keep the mind focused on the specific tone or "beats" that is being played.
- *Affirmation meditation.* This meditative technique uses affirmations to plant a certain way of thinking or to generate particular feelings within a practitioner's mind. The message is received and sinks in better to your brain. During affirmative relaxation, positive affirmations linked or connected to a specific area, such as health, relaxation, mood, or confidence, will be stated. Every time you want to embark on a relaxation technique, do the following:

1. Select a silent location with no disturbance.
2. Get into a comfortable position, sitting or lying down.
3. Loosen your clothes and free your arms and legs.
4. Dim your lights.

Mastering these relaxation techniques will take time. As time elapses, your body will be in sync and acclimatized with the process of relaxation methods. Once you master this, you will have the power to achieve intense relaxation. Make these practices part of your lifestyle, and do them daily. It is not easy to set aside time for meditation, but you can put these techniques into practice as you engage in doing other activities.

It is possible to meditate on a bus or while commuting for concentrative meditation. Mindfulness techniques can be put into play while walking or exercising your pet or while taking a lunch break at the park. Nonetheless, if you can designate a time daily for relaxation, do so for predictability and ease.

Do not try these relaxation techniques while sleepy as you will fall asleep and miss out on your target for relaxation. Relaxation requires maximum concentration and alertness. No one is perfect, especially at the beginning. Do not pinch yourself for missing some sessions. The main goal is to build momentum so that after a while you can get into a rhythm and routine.

Peace of Mind

Peace of mind is the key to a true life of being satisfied and content. Happiness, good health, and success should be accessed by every one of us. Meditation is among the paths to mental peace, which will open ways to a wholesome life. When we look at the many benefits of meditative practices listed earlier, they refer or are a testament to a state where one's body is in total control and fully functional. Bad habits are jettisoned for a purer health-conscious ones. Mental strength and brain functioning are greatly improved and nurtured. Immunity is boosted, leading to fewer or no diseases affecting us.

We are less stressed and a lot happier when we meditate regularly. Happiness and well-being are what spawn peace of mind; one becomes aware and in tune with themselves. Full self-awareness is achieved, and with that comes the peace. When your mind is peaceful, you will be more productive. You will relate better with people around you—your family, friends, colleagues at work, strangers that you bump into. You become more likable as the happiness and peace you exude rubs off onto others. Meditation, indeed, leads to peace of mind. Take up meditation, won't you?

Quick and Simple Techniques for a Beginner's Practice

Now that you have all the prior knowledge you need, it is time to delve into the practice itself. There are many kinds of meditation techniques that you can get acquainted with, and this chapter will aim to give you as many options as possible to help you start strong.

Fast and Simple: Techniques on the Go

There are just too many people out there who don't have enough time in their hands but still want to practice meditation. Although meditation can be done anywhere and in almost any circumstance, it is important that you start with some beginner-friendly practices that won't take up too much time. All the exercises in this section can be done within ten minutes, but you can make it last longer if you want.

When you are using certain techniques to fit a certain time frame, you have to put all thought of time constraints out of your head. It would be best if you chose a short time after you wake up or just before you go to bed. Keep in mind that making your mind be still is not easily accomplished, especially for a beginner, but also know that this can become simpler and easier as you go along, so don't let yourself be discouraged by any short-term setbacks.

Basic Meditation with Affirmation

This basic meditation technique is a great way to start your practice. This starts off with the basics, and you can add visualizations or added stillness later on.

Step 1. Have a seat or get comfortable on the floor. Ensure that your back is as straight as it can be but be careful not to strain yourself. Additionally, confirm that you are comfortable and can hold the position for not less than five minutes. Choose a place with no disturbance.

Step 2. Breathe intensely as you let your body relax. As this is probably your first time, it might be wise to keep your eyes closed throughout the process.

Step 3. Choose a phrase that you would like to affirm in your life. Try to use the first person and make sure it's something meaningful to you. Examples can include "There is peace inside me," "I am worthy of love," or "God watches over me."

Step 4. Take slow measured breaths. Make your breathing as easy and relaxed as possible and empty your mind of other thoughts.

Step 5. Now repeat the affirmation to yourself quietly. Try to focus only on the affirmation. If you do get distracted by random thoughts, allow the thought to pass rather than suppressing it. Simply and gently shift your focus back to the affirmation.

Step 6. In case you find trouble focusing with a purely mental effort, attempt whispering the words to yourself, moving your tongue without really speaking a word. Connect your breath to your affirmation and repeat the phrase as you exhale.

Go on with this process for five minutes or more. Remember not to get frustrated, as your body will end up tensing rather than relaxing. Don't forget how you feel while exercising. Was concentrating on affirmations and breathing a tough task for you? What kinds of thoughts did you find popping into your head?

Focused Breathing

When you can manage to stay focused on affirmations, it is time you focus solely on the breath. This is an awesome way of nurturing focused awareness, concentration, and calmness of the mind. Don't expect a quiet mind in an instant. This is all normal and will improve as you continue your practice.

Step 1. Find a comfortably sitting position, keeping your back straight in a place free from disturbance.

Step 2. Strongly breathe and let your body relax. Choose whether to close your eyes or not. However, if you find that your thoughts still have a tendency to race around you, keeping your eyes closed will help keep distractions at the minimal.

Step 3. Shift your attention toward the feeling of your breath. Feel your chest rise and fall as you breathe. Listen intently to the sound of each breath and feel the air enter and leave your body.

Step 4. Continue this meditation for five minutes or more. Since you are focusing solely on your breathing, you might find yourself easily distracted by random thoughts and emotions. Don't be alarmed and don't be critical of yourself when this happens. Simply acknowledge the thought or emotion without judgment, then let it go. Gently direct your focus back to your breathing.

It would be beneficial for you to continue practicing these techniques before you move on to more complex practices. As the basic core of almost all the meditation practices involves awareness of the breath and concentration, these techniques are great if you simply want to stay with the basics or if you want to move on and deepen your practice.

Rolling Up Your Sleeves: Longer and Deeper Practices

You can liken your mind to a deep lake. If you only look at the surface (the ordinary mind), you're often blind to the wonders underneath. When you start practicing focused awareness, you're actually learning to swim in the waters of your own mind. Once you start getting better at swimming, then you can start diving deeper into the depths.

This section will introduce more intermediate practices that allow you to get a good look into your own psyche. The exercises in this section should be done for twenty minutes or more. You can lengthen your practice time depending on your own preference and needs.

Body-Tuning Technique

This is one of the most vital intermediate techniques in meditation as it gets you connected back to your body. A large number of people in society are fragmented. The mind is often torn in fragments of positive and negative emotions that aren't fully explored. Worst of all, the body is disconnected from awareness and the mind. This technique aims to get the mind and body reconnected and to make them whole again.

Step 1. This meditation must be done lying down. Find a flat, solid surface that allows for comfort but not so much that you can end up drifting off to sleep.

Step 2. Shift your consciousness to your body as a whole. Pay attention to every sensation that you feel. Feel the places where your body touches the surface of where you're lying on. Feel the cool breeze that wafts through the room or the warmth of your own body.

Step 3. After spending some time in full-body awareness, gradually shift your attention toward the biggest toe on your left foot. Feel any perceptions in this specific area. If you have no sensations, then simply focus on the absence of sensation.

Step 4. Start to visualize your breath flow in and out of your toe, bringing much-needed energy with it. When you're ready, expand your awareness toward your whole left foot and continue inhaling and exhaling. Continue this for at least two minutes.

Step 5. When you're done, let your awareness travel upward to your ankles and lower leg. Be patient with yourself and continue visualizing your breath going in and out in waves across this area of your body.

Step 6. From here, go up to your knees and thighs. Once your left leg is done, revert down and concentrate on the other foot. Repeat the visualization and focus that you did on your other foot. From here, continue to go higher. From the pelvis, go higher to the abdomen, lower back, the navel, upper back, then the chest and shoulders.

Try to slow down in the areas where there are main organs, such as the lungs, heart, and stomach. Imagine your breath bringing healing energy to your organs. Now bring your focus to your left fingers and hands then up toward your elbows and arms. Repeat the same technique until you've finished with both hands. From here, bring your awareness to your neck then up to your face. Give special attention to the space right between your brows. Finally, finish by focusing on the top of your head. The last two areas can be especially receptive. You might end up feeling like you're floating and that your consciousness is more fluid in your own body.

Step 7. Once you're ready, shift your consciousness away from your head to the whole body. Feel your breath go in and out in waves.

Step 8. After a few minutes, wriggle your toes and fingers and slowly open your hand. Return your awareness to normal and stretch a little before you get up.

Meditation with Visualizations

Visualizations can be added to your basic meditation techniques and can help develop a certain trait or attitude in you. When practicing certain visualization techniques, simply start off with basic breathing meditation. When you feel at peace and still, you can start your visualization.

The Sanctuary

Visualizing a sanctuary or a refuge is a great place to recharge your energy and shake off some stress and anxiety. This technique can also help in healing certain mental and emotional wounds.

Step 1. Do your standard, basic meditation until your mind is relatively still and your body relaxed (preferably for five minutes).

Step 2. Start to visualize a place where you've always felt safe. It might be a real place from your past or just something you imagined. As long as it makes you feel safe and protected, then it should work. Be as specific as you want. If you imagine yourself in a garden, then what plants can be found there? Are there singing birds and trees that provide shade? Do your best to make the visualization as vivid as possible.

Step 3. Once you've found your safe place, simply allow the sensation of peacefulness, safety, and comfort permeate across your entire being. Know that you are safe here and that no one can touch you here. Within your sanctuary, you can explore all your emotions, even those of hurt, fear, and humiliation.

Step 4. Stay in your sanctuary long enough and ensure to end your session by reaffirming the positive emotions you perceive in your safe place.

Mindfulness, Anytime, Anywhere

Mindfulness meditation is practiced at any time while you are carrying out other activities. This is why mindfulness is one of the most preferred meditation technique on the go. Provided you completely focus on what you're currently involved with. You must have the ability to combine focused awareness with welcoming acceptance. The goal of this meditation technique is to have you fully present in whatever you're doing.

Mindful Eating

This is a great mindfulness exercise that you can do at work during your lunch break. Simply find a quiet place and eat your lunch.

1. Appreciate your food as you lay it out in front of you. Think of the effort and hard work that's gone into making your meal.
2. Look and smell. Note the appearance and aroma of your food. Be curious and notice everything you can see and smell.
3. Bring the food to your lips, and note how it feels against your tongue. Enjoy how the food tastes as you chew. Take note of all the emotions you feel as you eat.
4. Try to stay mindful throughout the entire meal.

Mindfulness can be done along with any other chores and activities as long as you practice focused attention. You can be mindful as you walk down the street or as you clean up around the house. You can even be mindful while talking to a friend or spending time with your family. Mindfulness can only amplify the joy and satisfaction that you feel as you engage in these activities.

Tips to Take It All the Way

You now have everything you need to start a practice, but what if you hit a few snags along the way? This section is about some user-friendly tips to help make your practice work for you. Here are little things you need to keep in mind to have a successful practice.

- Position: There are three basic positions you can take when meditating—namely, lying down, sitting up on a chair, or kneeling on the floor. Make sure to extend your spine as much as possible.

1. *Lying down.* Lie down with your feet hip-width apart, and let your feet fall naturally. You can place small cushions under your neck and knees for comfort.
2. *Sitting up on a chair.* It is important not to slouch or lean against your chair. Make sure that your buttocks sit a little higher than your knees so that your pelvis can naturally tilt forward. It is best if you use an old-fashioned wooden chair or bench.
3. *Kneeling.* This is thought to be the optimal meditation position. Because you are so close to the ground, you can become more in sync with the energies of nature and the earth, far from being the most stable position. However, it can be more difficult as it does take more flexibility and muscle strength. Research positions before you start if you want to consider kneeling. Try basic positions such as the easy kneeling position and the Burmese position before moving to the lotus position.

- Clothing: There are no special clothes you need to wear. You just have to make sure your clothes are comfortable and not too tight. Make sure what you wear won't distract you in any way.

- Location: Make sure the place where you meditate can accommodate the amount of time you need to finish your practice. Avoid places in the house that have a lot of "traffic," such as the kitchen, living room, and dining room. Eventually, you might want to create a special space with a meditation altar. This altar does not have to be associated with a certain faith or religion but simply hold all the items that are special to you. It can have incense, flowers, rocks you found in nature, and even pictures of your inspirations.
- Time: Basically, you can meditate whenever you have spare time. The best time for morning people is an hour right after you wake up. Being refreshed can help you be more focused and still than any other time. For those who aren't morning people, however, right after work or before bed are also good options as they can help relax you. The downside, though, is that you might already be distracted and exhausted from the events of the day. If you have the space, you can also try meditating during your lunch break if you find that any other time is not possible.

Quick Tips that can make Meditation Easier

- Star with the basics: Becoming too ambitious on your first try can leave you feeling overwhelmed. Try a five-minute basic meditation before you start doing a body-tuning technique just to test the waters first.
- Start within your comfort zone: Distractions can be your worst enemy when starting out, and doing a kneeling position that leaves you numb won't help. Start in a place, position, and time that are most comfortable with you. You don't have to follow the guidelines strictly if it causes pain. Be lenient and patient with yourself. If a position is painful, try a different one. Finally, by doing a few stretches on a daily basis, you will nurture the power to do even the full lotus.
- Distracting aches and itches: It can be hard to maintain a certain position if you know you have to stay still. Feeling little itches and aches can pop up when you still your mind. The best way of tackling this is to be fully conscious of the feeling. As you explore the sensation with curiosity and acceptance, you will find these little discomforts fade away. This is why meditation is often used as therapy for those who suffer chronic pain.

Chapter 4: Being Organized as a Minimalist

Just as we've discussed earlier, to be successful in minimalism, one has to be organized in everything they do. When one is considered organized, it simply means they are systematic and orderly in the way they approach and do things. Organization involves planning, managing your time well, and sticking to your plan.

Most of us will jot down a list of items to buy before we walk into a supermarket, or even if they do not, they will do a mental inventory of their supplies before making purchases. You set aside a day of the week for doing your laundry and house cleaning so that your house is kept tidy. At the office, we gather in the boardrooms to discuss and come up with strategies for propelling our companies or businesses forward.

Before you make that trip to Paris or a Safari to Africa, you inquire as to the costs, make bookings, and set a travel date. Before you send your daughter or son to school, you will make inquiries into a series of things before settling for a particular institution; of course—the place you feel will provide the best academic education for your child but also where your child will benefit from overall growth and development. When you are due for a job interview, you try to get to the place before the designated time, and by then, you shall have done a bit of research about the organization and, of course, familiarize yourself with the position.

The foregoing instances are all elements of organization—to plan in advance for an activity or event so that when you get to do what you planned for, it is easy, clear, and successful.

So why should you be organized? Experience and research studied have revealed that organized folks within the society are actually more inclined to succeed in whatever they do. They always achieve more as compared to disorganized people. This is because they seem to create more "free" time and lead happier lives. When you plan and follow the plan, you will be great at managing your life effectively and lead a fulfilling and happy life. By being organized, your time is well managed and your activities are planned, so there is predictability and thus ease of doing your things. You will always do things to completion, and your reward will be a happier life of satisfaction.

Therefore, if you are one who is not organized and always find yourself in a mess when handling things, you need to start planning and bring order to your life. All the time constraints and lateness or even the lack of idea about something you ought to know can be linked directly to deficiency or lack of organization. Next, let us look at the question of time and its management and why it is integral in your getting organized.

Know When to Say No

How often do you say no to an unscheduled meeting or a last-minute date? Do you recall the last time you declined the urge to a craving or urge to buy another handbag or run to the nearest Walmart to make purchases of items (most of which you already have or do not need) because of a slashed-price sale?

Being able to say no is an important component for you to get your life organized. Most often, we find ourselves bending over backward for family members, colleagues at work (especially our bosses), and friends to do things we had not planned to do because they asked us to. If you are a victim and you want to get your life in order, start saying no to activities that you have not planned for. The exception, of course, will be emergencies and very critical matters that may have been unforeseeable.

The moment you start tolerating unplanned or unscheduled activities, you will eat into the time meant for other things or leave some tasks uncompleted because you decided unwisely to compromise. You end up piling work or tasks that you would have otherwise finished with because you could not utter the word *no*!

Declining unscheduled tasks will free up so much time for you and relieve you of mental clutter and unnecessary workload. Try saying no from today and see how much easier your life will turn out. You will create enough time to do the most important activities you need to be concerned with—be it professionally, socially, or in your personal life.

When you already have a microwave that serves you well, say no to the impulse urging you to purchase another because it has a price-reduction tag on it. If your mother or sister did not let you in on their plan early enough, do not jump onto joining them simply because they called. Dedicate that time to doing the things you ought to be doing.

Once you learn to say no, always concentrate on a single activity at a time, like what we will discuss shortly. Multitasking is not necessarily the prudent way to go if your goal is to get organized.

Do One Thing at a Time

Concentrating on a single activity at a time means focusing on one issue and tackling it to completion before you embark on doing another. More often than not, we find ourselves bogged down by work or chores because we took on more than we could handle at one time.

Handling activities one after another means you will give all your undivided attention to the one you are handling; you will find yourself doing it much faster and better than having, say, five tasks to handle at the same time. Handling one activity at a time will make you more productive and resourceful. Filling your plate with a lot of tasks at a time will often result in one not completing some of the things taken on. However, if completed, you may find errors, or in hindsight, you may discover that you missed something that you would otherwise have not had you been concentrating on one.

You wouldn't want to be preparing food in the kitchen and watching *American Idol* simultaneously. You will find yourself missing a great performance while scampering to the kitchen or your onions burning because you got enthralled by a singer on the show. Similarly, you do not want to schedule an appointment at the same hour that you are doing a presentation. You will almost always not give one the adequate attention it deserves. You will come out as unprepared, disorderly, and unprofessional if you take this approach.

You will find yourself better organized if you decide to do one thing at a time; pressures of running late or not meeting deadlines will be greatly mitigated. This habit, if adopted and applied effectively, will realize more completions and success of tasks. Once you have resorted to doing one thing to completion then taking on another, I shall let you know the value of not procrastinating. Do that thing now, not tomorrow, not after ten minutes—*now*!

Do Not Postpone; Do It Now

Many people tend to defer tasks for "another time," ending up with piles of work with most not completed. Procrastination is a big enemy to achieving anything, and getting organized is no exception. Highly organized people do not postpone things that should be done; they do them there and then, and move on to the task that follows.

You need to actively nurture a trait of doing things as they are supposed to be tackled; postponing will get you in a rut of piling up work and not completing the stuff is important for completion. This habit can be very debilitating and can critically affect one's productivity if not nipped in the bud. For you to succeed in getting your life organized, start doing things now—not tomorrow or the minute after. By tackling and completing things when they are due, you avoid piling up work and become more productive. The more things you do on time without postponing, the more or better organized you will get, and the better your life is going to be. Next, we shall learn why that much-talked-about to-do list is important for highly organized people.

Keep a To-Do List

List down everything you intend to do in a book, diary, or any electronic device with the capability. A to-do list will help you get really organized if you adopt it in your day-to-day activities. Every highly organized and successful person has cited a to-do list as a compulsory component of managing their lives and is important in keeping them organized.

Once you have listed down the activities you need to take care of, the likelihood of forgetting something is not possible provided you utilize the list for the intended purpose of reference and priority of action. For purposes of good organization, one to-do list is recommended as keeping more than one can mess you up if one is misplaced or lost.

A to-do list can be done on a computer, your wall calendar, your phone, etc.; and with advancement in technology, the electronic devices come with reminder capabilities to help you not miss what you should do. Everyone who wants to get organized must keep a to-do list for reference; it is your planning log. Once you start keeping a list of activities, managing your day gets so much easier.

Advance planning is integral to getting organized, let's find out why next.

Plan in Advance

Advance planning will give you a head start for the next day. Always plan in advance if you want to elevate your life to the class of highly organized people. At the close of each day, draw a plan for your activities for the day that follows.

Schedule things to be done tomorrow this evening so that by the time you rest your head, you already have an outline of the things to do the next day and at what time. All the highly organized and successful people said that they plan things in advance, some even weeks in advance. Planning ahead gives your life predictability and enables you to manage your time much better.

To actualize self-organization, embrace advance planning and make it a habit to be ready ahead of time; you will rid your life of surprises and unnecessary pressures that may arise due to lack of foresight. The likelihood of being ambushed by duties or activities is significantly minimized by taking the simple step of planning ahead. Do this, and you will notice a big change for the better in the management of your life. Things will be a lot easier to accomplish since you are mentally prepared for them.

Planning ahead entails scheduling your activities for the future and putting time restraints on when to do them. Find out why schedules and deadlines are important if you are seeking self-organization.

Have Schedules and Deadlines

A schedule is a roster of things to do and at what times, while deadlines are the dates or times when the activities you have scheduled are due for completion. Everyone who wants to get organized must schedule their activities and put a deadline to all of them; otherwise, you will never attain an organized state. Schedules and deadlines are basically tethers that keep us in place and prevent us from wandering off aimlessly.

Lack of scheduling means no clear-cut things to do and will result in confusion and poor performance at what you do. Deadlines are important for time management while you are tackling your activities or duties wherever they may be. Without deadlines, most things would not be done at all, nor would they be completed on time.

Highly organized people keep schedules and set deadlines, which they abide by religiously; please adopt these two important habits, and you will change your life profoundly. While scheduling leave room for any last-minute things that may spring up, more often than not, important things that are not in your plans will arise. With schedules, you do not promise or overestimate what you will not deliver.

Next, we look at how to prioritize the items appearing in your schedule for better and optimal organization.

Prioritize

To prioritize things in your life means to categorize them from the most important to the least important and to pursue them in that order, with the most important being attended to first.

Knowing what is more important than the other is critical in the pursuit of self-organization; once you know the order of things in your life, then everything will fall in place quite easily. As one who is working to get organized, start prioritizing your daily activities for optimal performance and productivity. Start filtering through your to-do list and log them in their order of priority.

Tackling activities in their order of importance will save you from having backlogs or not finishing a task with a nearing deadline. Your order of priority could be hinged on the due date of the work, the quantity of the work, how critical it is, etc.

Once you prioritize things, then slot in "me time" as we shall discuss next.

Me Time

Organized people always set aside time for themselves where they have self-reflection and rest to rejuvenate and reenergize themselves. Me time is very important if you are working toward realizing your dream of an organized life.

Set aside time regularly where you spend time by yourself without the hassles of work or the attention of your home—just be by yourself. If you can dedicate a slot once every week to have your time, half a day or a full day would be ideal to achieve maximum results. Your time will help you clear your mind and have a clarity of purpose. Take up a relaxing activity during this slot; things like yoga and meditation have been proven to be great ways to get you relaxed. Do a bike ride through a quiet cycling track or take a walk in the woods or go to the spa for a relaxing massage and pampering session.

If can't afford to go out, you may decide to read a book that you really like or do a few rounds of swimming in the pool. It will surprise you how much better you will feel after one of these episodes and how productive you will transform to be.

Me time will give you the energy for a better-structured and productive life—an organized life!

Sleep

Lack of sleep is a major problem in our society. Insomnia is thought to be the number-one problem in the USA. More than 30 percent of Americans find it hard falling sleep each night, and half of the adult population say they have sleeping problems a few days of the week. Furthermore, almost half of those interviewed said that sleeping during the day affected their daily activities. These troubles are getting deeper and deeper with each passing day. Between the year 2000 and 2004, the number of grown-ups relying on sleeping pills was double. Also, the number of kids aged between one and nineteen who use sleeping pills rose to 85 percent.

Prescription drugs for inducing sleep reached 56 million in the year 2008. This is not something surprising in a society that worships productivity as well as activity. The current society is against rest and relaxation; we are constantly in a rat race. To us, getting rest translates to being glued on the TV, surfing the internet, or being occupied with some electronic device. Without enough sleep, you cannot be healthy. Why is sleep important for our bodies?

Sleep is responsible for the body's proper preservation as well as restoration of the neurological, endocrine, immune, and digestive systems. Melatonin increases naturally in the evening and aids in protecting us against infections. This is why one is likely to catch flu or cold if he or she fails to have enough sleep for a few nights. Sleep is so important that absolute deprivation of sleep has been proved to be fatal. An experiment in the lab showed that rats that are prevented from resting pass on within a period of two or three weeks. Having enough sleep has several benefits. The following are a few of them:

- Memory improvement
- Enhanced athleticism
- Boosting the overall mood and body energy

- Boosting immunity
- Increasing the stress tolerance

Having fewer than six hours of sleep daily is linked to low-grade persistent swelling and deterioration of insulin resistance. Additionally, it also raises the chances of being obese, diabetic, as well as developing cardiovascular disease. When are deprived of enough sleep, our thinking power, handle stress, and maintenance of a healthy system of immunity is greatly affected. Our emotions are also affected when we have less sleep. Here are the effects of being deprived of sleep:

- Weak immune system. Research conducted in the University of California revealed that less sleep weakens the body's immune system and affects its response to disease as well as injury.
- Addition of weight and obesity. Studies have shown that even a single night of sleep deprivation can lead to major changes in appetite and intake of food. Other studies have also shown that having less sleep affects carbs tolerance and sensitivity to insulin. Further, sleep deprivation leads to fatty liver disease.
- Reduction in awareness ability. Lack of enough sleep affects the short-term and long-term working memory and causes the degeneration of the nerve cells. All these negatively effects our thinking ability and make us function poorly.
- Emotion and brain health. Sleeplessness is linked to depression. Less sleep closes down the prefrontal cortex and can lead to several psychological conditions.
- Sleep deprivation also causes one to have a reduced life span.

Using sleeping pills can cause dependence, insomnia, drowsiness, memory loss, and much more. Medications for inducing sleep should be your last resort. To encourage yourself to fall asleep, you need to reduce your exposure to artificial light. Light that is not natural disrupts one's circadian rhythm and prevents sleep. A study revealed that the light released by alarm clocks and other digital appliances inhibits the production of melatonin. Here are tips to avoid exposure to light:

- Avoid being in front of a computer at least one hundred and twenty minutes before going to sleep.
- Make use of shades that can make your place of sleep darker.
- Turn off all digital appliances that glow or release any type of light.
- Use a sleeping mask if need be.

Also, do not eat too much or be too hungry before going to bed. An hour before midnight is better than having two thereafter. When you sleep, you experience a one-and-half-hour process of non-REM sleep, succeeded by REM sleep. However, the ratio of non-REM sleep within the half-hour cycles fluctuates through the night. Between 11:00 p.m. and 3:00 a.m., most of the cycles are consist of intense non-REM sleep and light REM sleep.

In the second half, between 3:00 a.m. and 7:00 a.m., the balance changes, and the process consists of more REM sleep, which includes dream time as well as a mild form of non-REM sleep. Staying late in the night is not good as our bodies are not tailored to do so. For ages, sleep patterns in humans have been linked with the daily variation in exposure to light. Our bodies are tailored to rise up in the mornings and go to bed at night, not the opposite way.

Several supplements that one can use to induce sleep exist in the market. One of them is magnesium. It is affordable and easily accessible. Melatonin is another hormonal supplement that can be prescribed to boost sleep.

Being Patient

Patience is being able to endure during tough times. It involves perseverance when provoked or when under strain. Furthermore, it means being able to keep your mind clear when in need. Patience is a major component of success, and for one to master it, it needs effort. These are the benefits when you are patient:

- You become better at making decisions. You will always take time to asses each and every situation, and you will know that rushing into decisions is not wise. You will have fewer chances of making mistakes as soon as you learn the benefits of being patient. When you are patient, you possess power. In short, patience is about having the right timing to act.
- You will be less stressed. You will understand that there are some things that take time and waiting for them to take place is not bad. When you are patient, you are less likely to be stressed, angry, or overwhelmed.
- You will be better at relationships. When you have patience, you will be more flexible and empathetic of the mistakes of others, together with their weaknesses. Moreover, you will have the ability to build relationships that are stronger and long-lasting. Patience and perseverance have a magical effect that will make difficulties disappear and obstacles vanish.

For you to have the ability to solve life's problems, you are required to fully understand them. This is why you are required to learn to be patient. Your patience originates from your childhood. The manner in which you used to cope as a child is not any different later in life. If you had a habit of throwing tantrums so that your parents could let you have your way, then your initial level of patience was low.

On the contrary, if you had parents that were strict but encouraging, you must have developed a different character and coped well with problems. This means that your initial level of patience was high. Patience is not something that comes overnight. You need to know that one has to develop patience over time and patience is built by patience.

How Can One Be More Patient?

- *Understand and counteract your triggers.* Impatience is something that is triggered; it does not just happen. The triggers are different from one person to another. You need to understand what your trigger is. Once you know what it is, you can do exercises or carry out techniques to calm you down whenever you feel the trigger building up.
- *Have self-confidence.* When one feels let down, loses control, or is overwhelmed, that is when impatience kicks in. You may want something to happen immediately but you seem not have the power of speeding up things. A person with self-confidence accepts situations as they are; he does not fight it but works with it. Patience and confidence go hand in hand.
- *Be positive.* Concentrate on the positive things in life, and avoid being negative-minded. By doing this, you will reduce tension and become happier. It is good to always turn a negative situation into a positive one.
- *Change your attitude.* Know that even if something happens later than expected, nothing will happen; it will get done, and everything will be okay.
- *Visualize.* Anticipate the expected problem and figure out how you will deal with it.
- *Relieve tension and stress.* Being impatient is the release of accumulated stress and anxiety. Always try to release stress and clean up your system.

Tips for Building Patience

- *Select a day that you make patience your goal.* Make an effort, take your time, and think about everything you do. When the day ends, make an observation of all the ways you made wise decisions and what you understood.
- *Take your time.* If you find yourself rushing around and trying to get things done in a hurry, stop. Before acting, take several deep breaths. Being impatient does not make things move faster in any way.
- *Practice delayed gratification.* Whenever you want to buy something, stop and think! Maybe you don't need it as badly as you think. You can save some money.
- *Think before talking.* At times, we talk without thinking about the consequences of our words. Pause and go over what you want to say to avoid hurting or offending other people.

Patience is a must when losing weight, attaining goals, having a baby, working out, excelling in your career, and many other situations. This is a valuable trait to nurture. It may seem passive, but it is actually a form of self-discipline.

Chapter 5: Happiness as a Minimalist

Lastly, happiness is important in minimalism. When you are happy, you will be organized and stress-free. Consequently, you will not accumulate clutter and buy things or spend time with people or doing things that are not important. The reason for living is to find out what makes us happy, get involved with them and enjoy life to the fullest. An example is that if there is a certain person that fills your life with joy and happiness, you need to try and spend more time with him or her whenever possible. In case you feel that your life is full of emptiness, you must carry out a self-assessment and figure out the reasons as to why you are not enjoying your life to the maximum. In the event you figure the reason for your happiness, then it becomes easier to be happy. If you discover something that makes you genuinely happy, then life will be better for you. Focus on things that will make you happy in the long-term haul. It should be something that influences your entire life. It lights up a fire inside you, and it never fizzles out. If there is one of the emotions that a majority of people find elusive, then it is satisfaction. Without discriminating according to society, financial ability, and place of residence, happiness is recognized all over the world. Even though we are always seeking joy as humans, it remains a tricky affair due to its versatility, influences, and attributes varying that greatly vary from one person to another. While one person be so optimistic and hopeful in the middle of troubles, another can be swimming in a life of opulence and lavishness but still remain unhappy.

    We are living in an era of conflicting forces and ideas. This universe is obsessed with development and advanced civilization but you still find that there are millions of people within the society that go without food. The economy of every country and the world in general is rising at a quicker pace due to many progressive innovations in the sectors of agriculture and technology. Consequently, our natural habitat is under constant and gradual destruction. Countries achieve extraordinary milestones in financial gain yet, along the way, fall victim to serious issues such as smoking, diabetes, misery, and different hurdles that come with civilization and modernization. It has been proven time and again that material possessions on their own will never offer you a happy life. An example, the world's financial superpower, the country of America. The United States has achieved unrivaled monetary and innovative advancement over the past several decades but still, its citizens are not the happiest. On the contrary, anxiety levels are as high as never before, social and financial gaps between the rich and poor have also widened significantly. Moreover, there is also great decrease in social trust, far from hope, faith and confidence in the authorities being low. Happiness has reduced or at least remained almost constant over the several years of increasing economic growth. This is because matters pertaining to poverty, anxiety, ecological degradation, and misery amid significant growth have been given a cold shoulder and regarded as unimportant issues. They need our passionate consideration—and certainly so at this point in life and history.

Happiness is connected to how we feel. It is more than only a passing state of mind. We are emotional creatures and experience an extensive variety of feelings very often. Negative emotions, like anxiety and outrage, help us escape danger or defend ourselves. Positive feelings—for example, delight and trust—help us to associate with others and construct our ability to adapt when things turn out badly. Attempting to carry on with a happy life is not about denying negative feelings or pretending to feel comfortable constantly. Every person experiences bad moments, and it's totally normal for us to feel anger, bitterness, dissatisfaction, and other negative feelings as an outcome. Happiness is a desirable state of mind or well-being that can be personal or shared within a group. Every individual has his or her meaning of joy. For instance, few people feel that satisfaction comes from having a lot of cash, and some believe that happiness originates from things, such as having friends. Happiness can influence your well-being and the people around you, and it can make one live a fulfilling life.

Happiness is about having the capacity to take advantage of the good times and adapt adequately to certain terrible situations. One mainstream misinterpretation about happiness is that cheerful individuals are, in some way or another, more inclined to be lazy. However, happiness enhances people's motivations and helps them perform better.

Happy individuals are less inclined to take part in unsafe conduct. For instance, they will probably use safety belts and more unlikely to be victims of street accidents. Happy individuals are economically responsible. They save more money and have more control over financial decisions. Individuals who are more satisfied with life tend to have a positive influence on the community. They will probably get involved in democratic processes, like voting, and do community service. They additionally have more respect and appreciation for authorities and offer aid to other people. Happiness is also infectious; happy people are likely to make those around them happy. In recent decades, we have turned out to be wealthier yet miserable. The benefits of good earnings have been clouded by disparity and low standards of trust and social attachment.

The quest for happiness is by all accounts a major problem. Bookshelves are filled with books and magazines on the topic of happiness. It is a part of our regular life to seek happiness. Just as we look to encounter joy and maintain a strategic distance from physical pain, we look for emotional happiness and try to keep away from emotional agony. Passionate joy, or happiness, is an essential part of human nature.

Happiness is more than what a single paper could portray. Several people describe happiness as an emotion you feel when you realize that everything is precisely as it ought to be. Some characterize it as the condition that you encounter when you have achieved your objectives. And others term it as having internal peace. Characterizing happiness is not straightforward. Our aim is to describe how to be happy and to know the hindrances of joy.

Happiness is a subjective emotion. It implies that what could make somebody cheerful may not be of any significance to another person. One may get happy through riches; however, for another person cash cannot bring the feeling of happiness. You typically get cheerful when you get something that fulfills an unmet need that you have. For instance, if you are experiencing a financial problem, then nothing could satisfy you more than getting money. If you are alone, nothing can make you happy more than getting into a relationship.

Later studies in the versatility of the mind have proposed that the brain is more amiable to change than we once thought. Not only can the cerebrum change neural pathways and alter the manner in which it works, but parts of the mind can develop or contract based upon its utilization. For instance, utilizing MRIs, researchers have had the capacity to demonstrate that people who take part in reflection have brains that are different from individuals who have recently begun this practice. The mind action of these people is well charged and developed in the territories that deal with happiness. It shows that we can train our brains to be happier along these lines. The capacity of our mind to change in this manner is called neuroplasticity.

Constructive psychology, a new branch, seeks to discover what makes an ordinary life happy and why a few people are more content than others. Happiness is becoming a common subject in magazines and articles; everybody appears to have an opinion about it. Too much literature makes it hard to differentiate between genuine scientific proofs and layman psychology. Love, cash, friends, or material things? Several studies have attempted to link particular factors that specifically lead to satisfaction. Despite the fact that there are some links, few of the discoveries are reliable, primarily because different people value different things. For example, some may consider it attractive to live in a major city, while others long to live in the countryside. As opposed to looking at particular elements, constructive analysts have taken a good look at how individuals perceive those factors that make them happy.

Causes of Happiness

Hope. There is no doubt that optimism is an attribute that causes satisfaction, and even research demonstrates it. Optimism is being cheerful and certain that things will go well. Hopefulness helps us to forget the past and not fear the future. Optimism makes us strong in the midst of things that cause anxiety. Being optimistic is not living in denial but is having hope that things will work out. Denial is imagining that reality is not. Good faith is picking the positive in the midst of despair.

Bad encounters can make individuals cynical. It is hard to convince people who have had negative experiences in the world to be hopeful. Changing their mindset can help them see things differently. They can also change their perspective once they go through a good situation after the bad one. For instance, if a person has had a horrible relationship and after that has a good one, they can recover from the adverse effects of the first one and realize that situations can change. The neuroplasticity research demonstrates to us that the cerebrum changes because of encounters of security, just as it changes in situations of danger. In treatment, when dealing with individuals who are depressed, doctors look for thoughts that are negative and cynical. Cognitive behavioral therapy is based on negative thoughts.

Happiness is the exploratory term for joy and life fulfillment, or rather thinking and feeling that your life is good. Researchers depend fundamentally on studies to survey the happiness of people, but they have also supplemented these studies with other measures. An individual's levels of satisfaction are affected by both inner components—for example, personality and perception—and outer variables, like the area in which they live. Some of the significant determinants of happiness are a man's character, the nature of their social interactions, the areas they live in, and their capacity to meet their essential requirements. To some degree, individuals adjust to conditions so that after some time their circumstances may not have any impact on our happiness as much as one may anticipate they would. Researchers have focused on the results of happiness and have found that happy individuals will probably be healthier, live for many years, have better social interactions, and be more productive at work. People with higher levels of happiness appear to be more efficient and healthier compared to individuals who are depressed.

Since we all like joy and peace, we cannot afford to overlook their causes. As much as we adore the outcomes, we ought to likewise find the causes and conditions behind them. As much as we need to be happy, we need to find the reasons for happiness too.

Thankfulness. The basis of happiness is to convey more delight to our hearts and be thankful for who we are and what we have. More often we overlook what we have and focus our attention on what we do not have. We always look elsewhere without taking a good look at our wealth. We look for what others have and overlook our qualities. We should have more happiness and gratefulness for who we are and what we have. We're all such amazing creatures, and we should appreciate each other's weaknesses and qualities. We should value our qualities and appreciate and value each other and ourselves. The primary source of joy is thinking that it is not enough for us to feel happy without caring about others. Thinking and wanting others to be happy is called love. Boundless affection for others is the fundamental way for every living being to be happy. Without adoring others, one cannot achieve happiness. Love makes everything rich, lavish, and indispensable. Love actually sparkles on everyone like the sun. With love, we turn everyone into a friend, and our brains become exceptionally calm and tranquil. Love is something we can encounter for ourselves. With adoration, we see everybody as unique, wonderful, and flawless, both outside and inside. We cannot see this as a result of our constrained inclinations and vision. However, everybody has exceptional beauty. We rely on others in our daily lives. We exist for others, and we have an obligation to love everybody.

If individuals list what they need most in life, happiness is quite often on the list, and most of the time, it is at the top of the priority list. When parents list what they need in life for their kids, they often specify health and material possessions, but happiness is always constant on the list. Parents often argue that whether their children are rich and occupy prestigious positions or not, they simply need their children to be happy. Happiness is one of the most important needs of individuals, if not the most vital. Happiness results from certain inner and outer causes, and thus it affects the way people live and their psychological states. Happiness is a beautiful thing and a critical variable in our future achievements. Since researchers have created accurate methods for measuring satisfaction, they have come up with causes and inhibitors of happiness.

Compassion. Another reason for joy is sympathy or compassion, which is the exceeding expression of our love. Sympathy is the desire and action to calm the anguish of others. When somebody we adore is in despair, we feel empathy and need to offer assistance. Each human being encounters troubles and distress. Nobody can avoid that. Compassion and empathy help us connect with others in their difficult circumstances. We keep them company and share their experience, their troubles, and their suffering. We give support depending on our abilities, causing us to feel happy, grateful, and satisfied. If we have strength, responsibility, and determination, slowly our abilities will develop, and our compassionate exercises will increase. If we become tired with others, it takes our chance to build our strength, affection, sympathy, and intelligence.

Another reason for happiness is *being appreciated*. Rejoicing in others' satisfaction is good since it reaffirms and reinforces our love and sympathy. When we adore somebody and they encounter moments of joy and peace or they are relieved of agony and troubles, it's a reason to celebrate. Feeling jealous and envy toward the success of others is a cause of unhappiness.

Money. A particular level of income is needed to address our issues, and poor individuals are most of the time disappointed with life. However, having a lot of cash has no effect on satisfaction in the long term. Well-off countries have a tendency to have higher levels of life fulfillment than developing countries, yet the United States has not encountered a rise in life satisfaction over the previous decades, even as the economy has grown. Research demonstrates that materialistic individuals have a tendency to be less happy, and putting your focus on family and different areas of life other than just cash is a wiser technique. Money can help in life fulfillment; however, when a good number of other profitable things are relinquished to pursue money, it results in unhappiness.

We have read stories of rich individuals who are troubled and of poor people who are exceptionally happy. For instance, several rich individuals across the world have committed suicide in recent times due to depression. On the other hand, a few people with ordinary earnings are very happy since they have figured out how to live within their means and appreciate the little things in life.

Family and friends. An association with family gives a specific kind of social support that you cannot get from strangers. If we are close to our families, we can rely on them in times of emergency and emotional stress. We can even rely on our families for financial support when we are urgently in need. We share our history and the future with the family. Our parents, guardians, and other close relatives can remind us of our childhood moments. This association with memories helps in times of emergency. It is because of genuine love that our family gives us joy and helps us during times of need.

Many years of research in happiness have revealed that the number and nature of a man's social interaction with friends, relatives, and neighbors are firmly connected with health and personal happiness. Individuals with many friends are less inclined to experience loneliness, stress, poor self-esteem, and issues like eating disorders and sleeping.

In the modern world, online networking, such as Twitter and Facebook, makes it easier to be connected with a large number of individuals. Many people live in communities that cherish privacy over closeness and relationships. Americans like homes where they can go for days without seeing their neighbors. Physical confinement is a recipe for loneliness and breeds sadness. Showing our children to value and cultivate close relationships is better than isolating them from neighbors and friends.

With regards to happiness, our closest and dearest truly matter. Research demonstrates individuals who have stable relationships with friends, family or other relatives are more satisfied, more productive, and live for so many years. Surprisingly, we regularly underestimate our closest family members. Keeping up with them requires close attention and effort. Social ties are critical in every aspect of our lives, from birth through to maturity. There is evidence to prove the positive effects that social links have, not just on our joy and mental performance but also on other aspects of our lives. It makes it necessary for us to connect with our family and friend. Our family links are the most vital of our relationships. Our wide family links enhance our satisfaction by making us feel more connected, giving us a feeling of belonging and self-confidence. It is the nature of our relationships that is vital, not the amount of relationship that we have. Indeed, poor relationships can be a cause of emotional stress and pain and can negatively affect our success. Finding a way to make and enhance our close relationships is crucial. Social interaction can be an incredible cause of joy. A day spent with loved ones is enjoyable and can be a source of memories for a long time to come.

It becomes easier to be involved with the daily hustles and forget what makes you happy. Ensuring your happiness level is higher can give you many health benefits. Happy people have healthy hearts and good arteries, and they are strong. Happy individuals recuperate faster from surgery, react well to stress, have normal blood pressure, and live longer than sad people. Studies also show that happy people may have strong immune systems, and they are less likely to get colds and other infections. Even when they get infected, their side effects are always mild. Happy people are good at taking care of their health as well. If people are happier, they practice more and go for checkups.

We are all aware of the saying that money cannot purchase happiness. However, we all spent money, making it a constrained resource. In what manner would we be able to spend our hard-earned money in ways that will raise our happiness? Research in psychology offers some helpful insights into the connection between money and happiness for us to think about before we spent it.

Being wealthy is not the route to happiness, as many people have been made to believe. However, money is still necessary for happiness. Having a higher salary, for instance, can give us access to homes in more secure neighborhoods, excellent health services and food, satisfying work, and more recreation time. However, this works up to a particular point. Once our wage gets to a particular level, our requirements for nourishment, medical services, security, and safe house are met. The beneficial outcomes of money—for example, purchasing comfortable homes—are often counteracted by the negative impacts, for instance, of working for long hours or being in a frustrating job to maintain the lifestyle.

Material things—for instance, the most recent iPhone or car—last longer than taking a piano class or going for the holiday. Purchasing material things make us cheerful in the short term. Over an extended period, however, we get used to new things, and despite the fact that they make us feel happier, in the end, they turn into normal. The satisfaction that originates from experiencing things, however, tends to increase over time. One cause is that we regularly share our encounters with other people. Despite everything, you'll be recounting stories with your family and companions about that time you went on vacation.

For you to be happy, think about spending money on the less fortunate in your society. Many people imagine that using the money on themselves will make them more content than using it on other individuals. However, when researchers evaluate satisfaction prior and then after individuals spend money, individuals report more happiness when they spend money on others or giving it to charitable organizations than when they spend it on themselves. One cause behind it is that providing for others makes us feel better about ourselves.

Physical exercise. Exercise is always touted as a cure for most things in a man's life, from stress to memory lapse. Exercise also makes us sleep better and feel more relaxed. Majority of us know about what happens to the body when we work out. We form more muscle and stamina. We are aware of how everyday exercises, like climbing stairs, get simpler if we work out frequently. When we work out daily, our mood becomes enhanced.

If you begin working out, your mind takes it as a time of stress. As the pressure of the heart increases, the mind assumes you are either battling stress or escaping from it. To shield yourself and your mind from stress, you discharge a protein called brain-derived neurotrophic factor. This brain-derived neurotrophic factor has a defensive component that improves our memory and enhances our mood. When you practice in a way that makes you strong physically, you also get mentally tougher. When a person is mentally stronger, he or she can deal with more stress. People can train by running, cycling, and other workouts. This mental strength also helps us in other parts of our life.

There is another method for diminishing anxiety and enhancing the state of mind that appears to make individuals more content, and it yields positive impacts more helpful for long-term satisfaction. When people take a walk, run, cycle, or take part in some other type of physical activity, they most of the time appear to feel more satisfied and less stressed. People in poor physical shape are not happy. One study at Stanford University in students found that happiness in a group is because of their identity rather than their athletic ability; however, there are parts of physical health that enhance pleasure.

Apart from feeling energized, physically fit people may feel a sense of achievement in meeting individual wellness goals. Additionally, they may feel pleased with the enhanced physical appearance that those hours in the exercise center have delivered. Furthermore, working out enhances the psyche and excites an otherwise dull day. There is a link between physical activity and happiness. Physical activity appears to increase sleep and reduce anxiety. Happiness and activity are identical in two remarkable ways: both are connected with enhancing the immune system and reducing stress.

Religion. For quite some years, people have been surprised by life. Thousands of years ago, Aristotle argued that the reason for man's existence is to be happy. Happiness is a major subject in different religions of the world. Man battles on his way toward happiness and paradise. Religion says that life itself is a blessing that must be valued. The scriptures say that we should celebrate and be cheerful. We ought to enjoy everything in life—spiritual, family connections, and material things. For Catholics, satisfaction is not just enjoyment. The best happiness is accomplished after death. However, good moral conduct in life can lead to joy and satisfaction. Muslim and Buddhism, too, view happiness in a moral way, where good behavior leads to happiness and success. As indicated by Bukhari, a scholar in Islam, genuine happiness does not come by having a lot of riches, but rather genuine happiness is the enhancement of the spirit. For Buddhists, joy is an internal feeling, a condition of the mind. Happiness can be accomplished in life by moral conduct that incorporates regard for others and having empathy.

Many people get happiness from religion. Are religious individuals more satisfied with life than nonreligious guys? And why is this case? Most studies have sought to find out if people are happy instead of studying causes. Studies have found that individuals who are involved in religion report higher levels of happiness than the individuals who are not religious. Church participation is a method for measuring religiousness. Scientists have analyzed how spiritual encounters are related to satisfaction. Religious encounters, especially when they happen during prayers, have been the most reliable indicator of happiness in some studies.

Religious participation is a channel for getting social support. People are more content when they are around other people. Religious gatherings tend to offer social support. This notion is backed by the trend of religious individuals being more satisfied with life. Religious guys feel a close association with God, making them happy. Joy and life fulfillment rise when we have a feeling of where we are going and what is vital to life. Apparently, many guys discover this in religion.

Religious encounters can be extremely positive. They offer us a sense of being in contact with God and contact with others. This is a positive thing, and obviously, if somebody is involved in positive things, they will tend to feel more satisfied than people who are not. There are three basic methods for connecting religion and joy. Sadly, research around there is correlational, implying that we cannot claim that religion leads to happiness.

Understanding the way of satisfaction is a contentious new theme in science. It shows up in all the experimental magazines, and television programs have been set up to discuss the subject, talking with researchers from everywhere throughout the world. The researchers have been attempting to see how the distinctive components of happiness and delight work in the mind. From their research on the topic, researchers have found that a lot of things we think will cause us to be happy do not make us happy, and even if they do, it is always for a short term. For instance, they discovered that money, sufficiently enough beyond catering for basic requirements, does not make people happy. Or even things cash can purchase. Research has demonstrated that even individuals who win large sums of money in a jackpot, after only a couple of years, become hopeless. In the first place, the things that give us joy are normally physical. Sex gives us substantial satisfaction. Cash and protests give us mental delight. However, all these things give short-lived joy. Before long, we underestimate things, including individuals, even things that once made us joyful. For instance, even if we have a new partner or a new auto or house or a new dress, the underlying rush soon wears off; and afterward, we begin searching for something better. We adjust to things so quickly, and the more goods and achievements we have, the more we need to continue raising our level of joy.

Happiness is different from pleasure. Pleasure originates from things. Happiness does not come from things; it is unconditional. It is a condition of being that originates from inside a person. Happiness is that state when there is no craving for something, only an appreciation for what a person already has. Happiness is a permanent feeling. If you have an appreciation for others and yourself, you have satisfaction.

As indicated by researchers, satisfaction is a highly attractive state. Proof demonstrates that cheerful individuals live longer than miserable people. They are also healthier and stronger and produce more results than others. In one study by the University of Illinois, the distinction in years lived was nine years between the happiest people and the unsatisfied individuals. Given that cigarette smoking can reduce a couple of years in your life, it makes nine years quite a long time.

Scientists give four keys to concentrate on while developing happiness. Obviously, the objective is not to bring happiness only but to transform our entire life. Scientists argue that as we begin to focus on ourselves and become less focused on outside things, happiness comes naturally.

Researchers demonstrate that kinship has a much greater impact on satisfaction than an individual's salary. It is not only on happiness but also on individual well-being; it is because our brains control a large number of components in our bodies that cause disease. Just as anxiety can trigger sickness, it looks as though friendship and satisfaction can enhance our defense against disease. Life gives us a chance to make friends. We always need to make a lot of friends in our life, sending warmth of friendship around. One strategy is to do a couple of things for others daily for which we do not expect any favors in return. Performing acts of kindness to others is one of the principles toward happiness.

There is always compassion even in bad people, and if you are loaded with compassion, you would have sympathy for others. Pity is not the same as compassion. Pity makes us feel better than others and desire to help or change them somehow. Sympathy includes affection and acknowledgment of individuals as they are. If people have compassion for others, they will know how to share happiness with those around them, and that will build happiness inside them. Compassion is not the same as pity. Pity makes us feel better than others, but compassion helps us share in others' misery.

Misery is a habit that is cultivated in someone's life. Happiness can likewise be developed as a habit. We simply need to begin searching for the things in life that are filled with light and not sadness. The way we view life influences what grows inside us. When we see joy and light all over, we will feel brilliant and satisfied. Life in itself is empty. Everything relies on how you view it. Letting go of sorrow and saying yes to happiness is key. Physicians have likewise found the advantages of happiness. Doctors have found out that happier patients recover fast than those who are sad. There are such a large number of things in life to be appreciative for, and when we focus on this stuff and express appreciation, it will change our life massively. We will be loaded with so much peace and happiness.

Showing appreciation for things in life is essential to happiness. Keeping an appreciation diary in which you consistently record things for which you are grateful for is important. Individuals are attempting, in each conceivable route, to get happiness via the body. The body can only give you temporary happiness, and agony follows every joy in the same degree. Sadness trails every delight. Death trails life pretty much as the day is trailed by night and life. It is an endless circle. A person's pleasure will be followed up by agony. When your happiness relies on worldly things, you will never be calm. When in happiness you get worried about the possibility of losing it, that fear will compromise your happiness.

Happiness is a very different thing than many of us think. It is always more of quality and less of quantity; it is more of a mental state, less environmental. The people who appreciate music nature and other life experiences are happier. Appreciating what we never had before is essential for our happiness.

Self-change frequently has a bad effect on our emotions. When you do not accept who you are, you end up dismissing yourself as a failure. Your brain instantly makes a picture of what you ought to be, and another part of your brain discovers that you are not what you are supposed to be. Your mind makes a conclusion that you are not good enough because of not meeting the goals you have set.

By coveting to be something else, you create a mental image of what you ought to be, and you intuitively dismiss yourself in your current shape. An example of self-improvement is weight reduction. Weight reduction is likely prompted by the conclusion that the body is not in good shape and that, therefore, we need to change. The more you do not like body, the more committed you will be in losing weight. Getting fitter leads to self-acceptance. The point here is that the body never causes unhappiness, but the self-rejection in your brain does.

Self-acceptance. Self-improvement is a developing industry, and it's no big surprise; a significant number of its customers never end up happy and satisfied because they kill their motivation and self-esteem through rejection. On the other hand, they achieve their objectives just to discover they haven't managed the rejection in the mind bringing about the unhappiness. Promotion does not change self-rejection. Researchers have demonstrated that material things do not influence a man's satisfaction in the long term. Joy does not come from material things or achieving certain milestones in life. Rather, it comes from the ability to express ourselves and influence those around us.

People do not need to change themselves to be happy, but rather, they need to change the emotions they express. When people express outrage, they feel angry. If people exhibit love to others, they feel love and happiness about themselves. We frequently relate feeling satisfied with what we have. The material things do not make us happy. It is the love and compassion we show others that make us happy.

Happiness has always been associated with people spending time with people they cherish and dealing with things they love. The basic thing for happiness is not what they accomplish. The thing that makes them happy is expressing love in whatever they do. Accepting oneself is the initial step toward showing love for yourself. Attempting to be something other than what you are creates a feeling of self-rejection. The brain's way of avoiding self-rejection is just accepting yourself. This method reduces self-rejection and restores a feeling of self-worth.

Happiness is not assured just because you accomplish your life goals. They are just illusions we create in the brain to trigger feelings of joy. It is what we express at a moment that determines the satisfaction and happiness in life. When we express love, we become happy. When we express feelings of displeasure, we become sad. The way to get true satisfaction in life is to express love. Since expression of affection is under your control, you have the key to happiness.

We always get messages about what makes us happy in life. Marketers tell us it originates from owning and using their items. The media tell us it comes with riches and popularity, while the government thinks happiness comes from a growing economy and rising standards of living. For so many years, we have used philosophy, religion, and history to seek answers to such questions; however, in the recent past, analysts have contacted scientific research on the subject.

Researchers have discovered that despite our genes and circumstances having a role to play in our happiness, so much of our happiness originate from our decisions and the exercises we do. So despite the fact that we are unable to change our inherited attributes or the situation in which we get ourselves, we have the ability to change how happy we are in the way we approach our lives.

Despite the fact that everybody has a brain, a large number of us have little comprehension of its functions and capacities. For instance, if we have no training in Dharma, we might know very little about the distinctive parts of the brain, the way they are formed, and the impacts they cause in our lives. We cannot have the capacity to recognize virtuous brains from a non-virtuous one. Why is it important to comprehend this? The purpose is that happiness relies on the brain, and if we need to avoid anguish and discover genuine satisfaction, we have to comprehend how the brain functions and utilize that knowledge to control our brain. It is only this way that we would we be able to enhance the quality of our life, both now and later on. Whatever issues we encounter, they originate from our mind.

Lately, our comprehension and control of the outside world have increased significantly, and therefore, we have witnessed unprecedented material creation; however, there has not been a corresponding increase in happiness. There is no less suffering on the planet today, and the problems have increased. In fact, it may be said that there are currently more issues and more suffering than witnessed before. This proves that the reason for happiness and the answer for our issues do not lie in control of the outside world. Satisfaction and happiness are states of the mind, thus their primary source is in the brain. If we need to be really happy and free from anguish, we should enhance our comprehension of the brain.

Very often, when things turn out badly in our lives and we experience bad situations, we tend to view the circumstance itself as the issue, yet in truth, whatever issues we encounter originate from our brain. If we react to troublesome circumstances in a positive way, we might not have problems; we are supposed to view them as chances for development and advancement. Issues emerge only when we react to problems negatively.

Be aware of the body's signals. The body communicates through signs of comfort and discomfort. Before engaging in a certain behavior, think about how you will feel. If the body feels physical pain, take care. Forget the past, live in the present, and stop worrying about the future. Maintain your thoughts on the current situation. Maximize each moment. Accept what happens, appreciate it, gain from it, and let it go.

Take a moment of silence to contemplate and calm the inner soul. Take into consideration your internal thoughts so you can be guided by instinct instead of the worldly interpretation of things. Do not value external approval. You are the judge of your value, and your objective is to find worth in yourself, regardless of what any other individual thinks. When you end up reacting to situations with anger, understand that you are just battling with yourself. When you surrender the anger, you recover from situations.

Pay little attention to judgment, and you will feel much better. Anything can be forgiven; however, when we pass judgment, we fail to understand and love others. In passing judgment on others, you exhibit self-rejection. When we forgive, we improve our self-esteem. Do not use things that are bad for your health. Your body is the one that supports your happiness. The strength of each cell contributes to your happiness. Be motivated by love rather than fear. Fear results from a mind that refuses to move on from the past. Remembering what hurt us in the past makes us think they will happen again.

Unhappiness is an unavoidable part of life. It is an ordinary reaction to physical and mental misfortune. Everybody is influenced uniquely by outside and individual issues that may incite unhappiness. Unhappiness is not a mental problem; it is a feeling that may last a couple of minutes or a couple of days. Sometimes it surfaces after quite a long time. Changes that lead to loss of dignity and reliance on others cause unhappiness. The changes happen with ailments, like heart disease. Hormone changes, for example, increase production of estrogen before female monthly periods, and pregnancy may likewise cause unhappiness. Unhappiness is a response to emotional and social misfortune. An example of misfortunes includes the death of a friend or family member, loss of a job, and poor health. Unhappiness is also brought about by a yearning for impossible things. Nostalgic feelings also bring about a situation of unhappiness.

When you come across a person who is unhappy, you also react with a sad expression and words. When you know individuals or creatures are going through pain (whether in your area or different parts of the world), you may encounter emotions of sadness. Some individuals are vulnerable to unhappiness than others. Elderly people encounter periods of unhappiness than the younger ones. Research in brain science shows that music may cause unhappiness. Analysts found that people who listened to sad music were unhappy because it evoked nostalgic memories. However, those who listened to happy music reported fewer episodes of unhappiness.

Conclusion

It is ironic that a book on minimalism is quite a lot of pages! The reason is that I wanted to offer you, my reader, a comprehensive guide on how to live as a minimalist. Anyway, thank you for taking the time to read this informative and educative book on minimalism. Inside here you have learned what minimalism is and its barriers. We have discussed ways of avoiding these barriers for you to live a satisfied life without the urge to acquire and do things that are not necessary in your life.

Minimalism will enable you to focus on what's essential in your life. You will be able to pursue your dreams, develop healthy relationships, and improve your health. The key is to be organized, to manage your stress, to find ways of being happy other than acquiring and hoarding stuff, and lastly, to spend some alone time reflecting and meditating about life.

© Copyright 2019 All rights reserved.

The content contained within this book may not be reproduced, duplicated or transmitted without direct written permission from the author or the publisher.

Under no circumstances will any blame or legal responsibility be held against the publisher, or author, for any damages, reparation, or monetary loss due to the information contained within this book. Either directly or indirectly.

<u>Legal Notice:</u>

This book is copyright protected. This book is only for personal use. You cannot amend, distribute, sell, use, quote or paraphrase any part, or the content within this book, without the consent of the author or publisher.

<u>Disclaimer Notice:</u>

Please note the information contained within this document is for educational and entertainment purposes only. All effort has been executed to present accurate, up to date, and reliable, complete information. No warranties of any kind are declared or implied. Readers acknowledge that the author is not engaging in the rendering of legal, financial, medical or professional advice. The content within this book has been derived from various sources. Please consult a licensed professional before attempting any techniques outlined in this book.

By reading this document, the reader agrees that under no circumstances is the author responsible for any losses, direct or indirect, which are incurred as a result of the use of information contained within this document, including, but not limited to, — errors, omissions, or inaccuracies.

www.ingramcontent.com/pod-product-compliance
Lightning Source LLC
LaVergne TN
LVHW020429070526
838199LV00004B/336